FINDING YOUR PURPOSE

A Guide To Personal Fulfillment

Barbara J. Braham

A FIFTY-MINUTE™ SERIES BOOK

CRISP PUBLICATIONS, INC.
Menlo Park, California

FINDING YOUR PURPOSE
A Guide To Personal Fulfillment

Barbara J. Braham

CREDITS
Editor: **Elaine Brett**
Designer: **Carol Harris**
Layout and Composition: **Interface Studio**
Cover Design: **Carol Harris**
Artwork: **Ralph Mapson**

Copyright © 1991 by Crisp Publications, Inc.
Printed in the United States of America

English language Crisp books are distributed worldwide. Our major international distributors include:

CANADA: Reid Publishing Ltd., Box 69559—109 Thomas St., Oakville, Ontario Canada L6J 7R4. TEL: (416) 842-4428, FAX: (416) 842-9327

AUSTRALIA: Career Builders, P. O. Box 1051, Springwood, Brisbane, Queensland, Australia 4127. TEL: 841-1061, FAX: 841-1580

NEW ZEALAND: Career Builders, P. O. Box 571, Manurewa, Auckland, New Zealand. TEL: 266-5276, FAX: 266-4152

JAPAN: Phoenix Associates Co., Mizuho Bldg. 2-12-2, Kami Osaki, Shinagawa-Ku, Tokyo 141, Japan. TEL: 3-443-7231, FAX: 3-443-7640

Selected Crisp titles are also available in other languages. Contact International Rights Manager Tim Polk at (800) 442-7477 for more information.

Library of Congress Catalog Card Number 90-83475
Braham, Barbara J.
Finding Your Purpose
ISBN 1-56052-072-8

This book is printed on recyclable paper with soy ink.

PREFACE

WARNING!

The book you are about to read could change your life. There are many questions you will ask yourself as you go through life, but there are none more basic, more fundamental, more critical than ''Why am I here? What is my purpose?'' To answer these questions is to face the mystery of your life. If you are willing to take this risk, this book is for you!

When you asked yourself the question, ''What is my purpose?'' you embarked upon a journey of personal and spiritual growth. It is a rewarding and difficult journey. In the following pages you will be asked tough questions. If you are to benefit fully from this book, you must have the utmost personal integrity. Will you commit to completing the exercises thoroughly and honestly? If you take seriously the process disclosed in this book, you may discover things about yourself that lead to significant changes in your life. People have been known to quit their jobs and change careers after completing these exercises. Some have moved to other parts of the country. Still others have married or divorced.

Finding Your Purpose is at once easy to read and extremely challenging. You can skim through the pages in about an hour; the exercises take you through your lifetime. If you are willing to face yourself at this intimate level, read on! You won't be disappointed.

Barbara J. Braham

i

ABOUT THE AUTHOR

Barbara J. Braham, MSW, is a speaker, facilitator, author, and consultant. She has delivered hundreds of seminars to Fortune 500 companies since starting her own consulting business in 1985. Her topics include ''Calm Down: How to Manage Stress,'' ''New Truths for the Nineties,'' and ''Finding Your Purpose.''

Formerly associate director of a multimillion-dollar mental health center, she facilitates corporate planning retreats as well as monthly retreats for individuals who want to find their purpose. She is the author of four books and two audiocassette programs. She serves as president of the Ohio Speakers Forum, a chapter of the National Speakers Association.

For information about her retreats or seminars, write to her at: 1143 Neil Avenue, Columbus, Ohio 43201, or call (614) 291-0155.

ACKNOWLEDGMENTS

Special thanks to:

Lynn Kiely, Ph.D.—this book is an evolution of our conversations over the past fourteen years.

Kelly Allen, Bill Bickham, Marilyn Bollinger, Kathy Hoyt, Judy Latshaw, Bill McGrane CPAE, and Mary Struble—for their review and feedback on the manuscript.

Jane and Granville Braham—for their love and support.

Rick Sullivan—for modeling everything I believe and being such a joyful companion on life's journey.

TABLE OF CONTENTS

TABLE OF CONTENTS (Continued)

CAN THIS BOOK HELP?

Are you wondering about your purpose? Read through the following questions and check those statements that are true for you. If you check more than six questions, this book can help you!

☐ 1. I sometimes feel that there is something missing in my life.

☐ 2. I don't feel much joy in my life.

☐ 3. I don't like what I'm doing for a living, but I don't know what else to do.

☐ 4. There's something I've always longed to do, but I can't find the courage to do it.

☐ 5. I believe I could contribute more than I do.

☐ 6. It seems like I spend my life doing what I "should" do instead of doing what I believe is right.

☐ 7. I don't ever seem to have any time for myself; I'm always busy.

☐ 8. I can relate to the song that asks, "Is that all there is?"

☐ 9. I have all the things that are supposed to make me happy, except I'm not happy.

☐ 10. I often compare myself to others, even though it usually makes me feel bad.

☐ 11. I wonder if being successful is really worth it.

☐ 12. It's hard for me to relax; I feel like I need to be doing something all the time.

☐ 13. I think about the questions: Why am I here? What's my purpose?

☐ 14. I believe that there has to be more to life than what I've been experiencing.

☐ 15. I try to make things happen rather than allow them to happen.

☐ 16. I am reassessing my spiritual beliefs.

☐ 17. I feel like there is something I am "supposed" to be doing, but I'm not sure what it is.

☐ 18. I want to make a difference in the world.

PART

I

What Is Purpose?

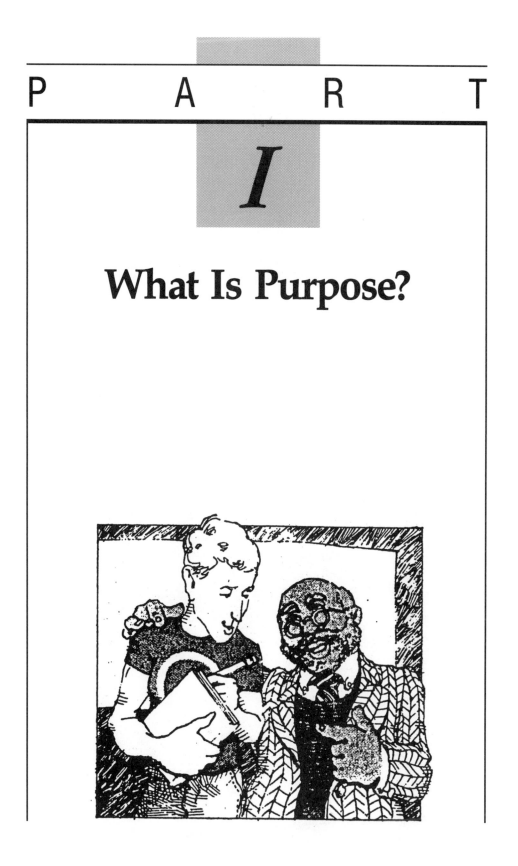

WHAT IS PURPOSE?

Every once in a while you meet people whose work is inspired. They exude enthusiasm. They appear to care genuinely about what they are doing, the people with whom they work, and the people they serve. They express a joy that seems to come from deep within; it's not forced or superficial. You sense their genuineness and authenticity, and you don't believe they are playing a role.

When you meet such people you realize that their work is consistent with their purpose. You might say they are working ''on purpose.'' They know why they're here, and they know the difference they want to make. This clarity and focus on their purpose makes them stand out from most of the people you meet.

Who are these people? They could be anyone—a teacher, parent, executive, artist, sales clerk, mechanic, social worker, or secretary; it doesn't matter what they do. What matters is that they do it from a centered purpose.

Job satisfaction and fulfillment come from the inside out, not the other way around. In other words, you can have two teachers who seem to do the same thing. Yet one has a job, while the other has an impact on children's lives. One feels stressed and burned out much of the time; the other feels excited, energized, and challenged. The difference between them is that one teacher is fulfilling his or her purpose, while the other is not.

Take a minute now and think of people in your life who seem to love what they do. Write down the names (or jobs, if you don't know the names) of three of these people. Then describe what there is about them that makes you think they know and live their purpose.

PEOPLE WHO LOVE WHAT THEY DO

Person #1: _____

_____

_____

Person #2: _____

_____

_____

Person #3: _____

_____

_____

WHAT OTHERS SAY ABOUT PURPOSE

Many authors have written on the subject of purpose, especially in the past few years. Each brings a unique voice to this common subject. As you read through these quotes, notice what they have in common and what makes them unique.

> In responding to vocation—the call, the summons of that which needs doing—we create and discover meaning, unique to each of us and always changing.
>
> Marilyn Ferguson, *The Aquarian Conspiracy*, 1980

> The "midlife" crisis with which the psychotherapists grappled probably reflects the fact that at midlife one's own death becomes less theoretical and more probable. Goals of money, security, fame, sex, or power might formerly have given purpose to life. With experience, the limited nature of such satisfactions becomes increasingly evident...the search for meaning becomes increasingly urgent.
>
> Arthur J. Deikman, *The Observing Self*, 1982

> The historic period in which we live is a period of reawakening to a commitment to higher values, a reawakening of individual purpose, and a reawakening of the longing to fulfill that purpose in life.
>
> Robert Fritz, *The Path of Least Resistance*, 1984

> My advice is to live your life. Allow that wonderful inner intelligence to speak through you....Follow your bliss and be what you want to be. Don't climb the ladder of success only to find it's leaning against the wrong wall.
>
> Bernie Siegel, M.D., *Love, Medicine and Miracles*, 1986

> But each incarnation, you might say, has a potentiality, and the mission of life is to live that potentiality. How do you do it? My answer is "Follow your bliss." There's something inside you that knows when you're in the center, that knows when you're on the beam or off the beam. And if you get off the beam to earn money, you've lost your life. And if you stay in the center and don't get any money, you still have your bliss.
>
> Joseph Campbell, *The Power of Myth*, 1988

A DEFINITION

Mission, vision, vocation, calling, bliss, meaning, passion—these are just some of the words that have been used to describe our human need to identify and express our purpose. Ultimately, finding your purpose is a spiritual quest. It represents your ability to connect with something greater than yourself. ''Why am I here?'' goes far deeper than what career is best for you. The remainder of this book will help you look inside yourself for your answers, which is the only place you will find them.

Throughout this book you will see the word *passion* used to refer to purpose. There are several reasons for this. First, look at the word carefully. You will see that it contains the very essence of what purpose is about:

Pass - I - On

Isn't that what you want to do—to make a difference in the lives of others and leave something of yourself behind? None of us wants to think that we have lived and died without leaving any trace of our uniqueness behind.

The word *passion* is also used because it is about feeling. To fulfill a passion is to express deeply held feelings. Passion is not intellectual or rational. It comes from the heart—a *calling* as Marilyn Ferguson would say. You don't think about what your purpose is, you feel or know your purpose. You don't figure it out, you experience it.

Passion implies desire, and your passion, if given a voice, will arouse you to take action. Once known, it demands to be fulfilled. If we fail to listen, we suffer stress, fatigue, frustration, or dissatisfaction.

Passion is compelling, it creates an inner sense of urgency quite distinct from the external events of our lives. Passion allows us to be truly alive!

Now that you've thought about people you know who are working on purpose and have read the ideas of others on purpose, what are your ideas about purpose? What words or phrases would you use to describe it?

To me, purpose is:

SYMBOLIZING PASSION

You might think of passion as a burning desire, which is one reason why a flame is used as a symbol. Sometimes it is easier to symbolize your passion than to try to describe it in words. Symbols are often richer and more vivid than words. They also speak to the right side of the brain, which is where your passion is experienced.

There are many reasons for choosing the flame as a symbol. A fire gives off warmth. When you are around people who are living their passion, you notice that they are warm. You can feel them reach out to their work and the people around them.

A flame is also bright with light. When you live your life from your passion, you too are a source of light. Throughout the ages, light has meant truth, wisdom, and knowledge. All of these are appropriate to a life lived with purpose. To follow your passion is to live your truth as you understand it from the inside, not to try to live someone else's truth. Many people try to live the truth of their parents, friends, or images they see in the media. This can only lead to dissatisfaction.

A fire is consuming and powerful. When you know your passion, you find that it can consume you. Ironically, that's the goal. George Bernard Shaw expressed it well when he said, ''I want to be thoroughly used up when I die....Life is no 'brief candle' to me. It is a sort of splendid torch which I have got hold of for a moment, and I want to make it burn as brightly as possible before handing it on to future generations.'' And your passion is powerful! Who is more powerful than the person who has a mission in life? Ghandi, Joan of Arc, and Martin Luther King were empowered by their vision. The depth of their vision inspired and empowered others.

Have you ever stared into the flame of a candle or a fire? You can easily become hypnotized by its flicker. After a time everything else disappears from your awareness and you seem to merge with the flame. This unity, or sense of oneness, is a reminder of the spiritual experience in which you are no longer separate from the world. When you are in complete alignment with your purpose, you will have a similar experience of oneness.

If the flame goes out, if you feel disconnected from your passion, you'll probably say you feel ''burned out.'' You can experience stress from time to time because you become sloppy in your living habits. But if you're burned out, you're probably living from the outside in. When that happens, your aliveness, your life force, feels snuffed out, dead. However, when you act consistently with your purpose, it's like adding fuel to the fire!

As you read through this book, stay alert to pictures, images, or symbols that come to mind for your passion. You will be asked to create a symbol for your purpose before you finish reading the book.

PURPOSE OR MEANING?

Is there a difference between these two words? Yes, there is an important distinction. You can have a meaningful life whether or not you believe you have a purpose. Meaning is the significance that *you* attach to an event, person, or situation. You can have meaningful work, no matter what you do, if you decide to assign it meaning. To ascribe meaning is a rational, left-brain act. A well-known story makes this distinction clear. Two stone masons were at work when a visitor came upon them. Curious, the visitor asked the first one what he was doing. He replied that he was cutting stone. Then the visitor moved on to the second stone mason and asked the same question. His reply was, ''I'm building a cathedral.'' The second man had given his work *meaning*.

Purpose is quite different. You do not bestow purpose. It is something that flows from deep within you. Purpose is the potential that you hold, much as the acorn holds the potential for an oak tree. Purpose is what you are called to do. It is a part of your uniqueness. Purpose is your expression of the divine.

Meaning and purpose are both important. Think about what gives your life meaning. Make a list of the people and things that are meaningful to you and why.

PEOPLE AND THINGS THAT ARE MEANINGFUL TO ME

People/Things	What They Mean to Me

YOUR MOST MEANINGFUL EXPERIENCES

Think back over your life and recall your most meaningful experiences. What happened? Why was that event important to you? What impact has the experience had on your life?

Experience #1

_____

_____

_____

_____

_____

Experience #2

_____

_____

_____

_____

_____

Experience #3

_____

_____

_____

_____

WRITE YOUR PURPOSE—
FIRST DRAFT

Before you read any further, write down what you believe your purpose is.
It is okay if it is vague at this point. It will become clearer as you work through
this book.

My purpose is:

WHY FIND YOUR PURPOSE?

From the time you are born until the time you die, you are growing and changing. As you go through life, there are specific developmental tasks you need to complete before you move on to the next stage. You are probably familiar with the developmental tasks of childhood and adolescence. When you reach adulthood it's easy to think you're through with these tasks. Of course you recognize that there will be changes: marriage, children, career moves, empty nest, aging parents, retirement, and so on. But you may not have related these external events to your internal emotional, psychological, and spiritual growth.

Midlife, roughly from your late thirties to your late fifties, is the developmental stage at which you need to come to terms with the meaning of your life. Carl Jung was one of the first psychiatrists to write about this period of life. He said, "Among all my patients in the second half of life—that is to say, over thirty-five—there has not been one whose problem in the last resort was not that of finding a religious outlook on life....This of course has nothing to do with a particular creed or membership of a church."

The largest segment of our population today is in midlife. Record numbers of them are asking:

Who am I?

What do I want to be when I grow up?

Why am I here?

If I'm so successful, why aren't I happy?

These questions are critical if you want to continue to grow toward self-actualization. And the questions are uncomfortable. Do you know people who have had an affair, bought a sports car, or found some other way to distract themselves from these questions? Have you been avoiding these questions?

IS YOUR PRESENT WORK YOUR PURPOSE?

Answer the following questions *yes* or *no*.

YES NO

☐ ☐ 1. Do you love what you're doing?

☐ ☐ 2. Do you find it easy to go to work most days?

☐ ☐ 3. Do work and leisure time sometimes seem the same?

☐ ☐ 4. Do you feel things are all right in your world?

☐ ☐ 5. At times when you feel frustrated or irritated with a particular aspect of your job, do you maintain a deep feeling that what you're doing is still "right"?

☐ ☐ 6. Do you feel there's nothing else you'd rather be doing?

☐ ☐ 7. Do you feel at peace in your life?

☐ ☐ 8. Do you trust that things will work out for you?

☐ ☐ 9. Do you have a positive attitude most days?

☐ ☐ 10. Does your work energize you?

DISCOVER YOUR PASSION

The culture and dynamics of the 1980s have given this developmental task an urgency unprecedented in history. The last decade was characterized by people living from the outside in—the opposite of following their passion. Money and what it could buy became equivalent to success. Did you get caught up in this shallow definition of success? If you did, then you may feel that your life is like a Lifesaver—there are many things, activities, people, swirling around the outside, but there is a hole in the middle. Your center—your passion—is empty. Joy and happiness can be found when you fill up your center.

Do you know people who hate their work? How did they get into that work? Often they didn't follow their passion. They let themselves be talked into it because it paid well, was close to home, or had good hours. All of these are important considerations....*after* you know your purpose. If they are the only questions that guide your decisions, you may find yourself unhappy and dissatisfied with your life.

It is important to note that your passion may not always be what you get paid to do. Your passion might be raising your children, for example, and you may need employment to support them financially. In this situation you might choose a job that is close to home and pays well. Working supports your passion; it is not your passion. If you can keep this clear, you won't expect your paid work to provide fulfillment and you won't be disappointed. On the other hand, you can make the work meaningful and bring joy and contentment into your life. Each yes answer on page 11 is an indication that your work and your passion are in alignment. When you can answer *yes* to all the questions, you are living your passion.

P A R T

II

The Five Masks

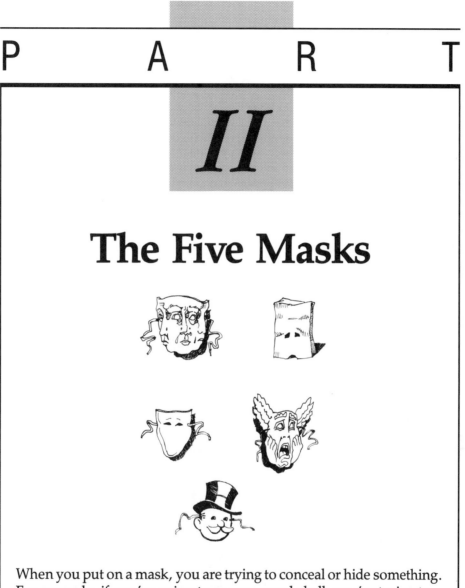

When you put on a mask, you are trying to conceal or hide something. For example, if you're going to a masquerade ball, you're trying to conceal your true identity. If you are exceptionally nice to someone, you may be masking negative feelings toward them.

You can also wear masks with yourself. That's what often happens with your passion—it is hidden from you by certain masks that you wear. In this section of the book you will learn about the five masks that may be concealing your passion. You may discover that you're wearing all five. Or maybe you wear only one. Until you can take off your masks, you may be unable to answer the question ''What is my purpose?'' You'll be given a specific prescription, or R, for how to remove each one of the masks.

MASK #*1*: *BUSYNESS*

The challenge to find meaning in what you do is at the core of the new work ethic. Employees want more than just a paycheck from their work. They want to feel connected to their organization's mission and vision. They look toward the organization as a place where they can grow and accomplish their own personal vision as well as the organization's larger purpose.

Cynthia Scott and Dennis Jaffe, *Take This Job and Love It*

MASK #1: BUSYNESS

Take a few minutes now to answer these questions.

How Busy Are You?

1. How many hours do you work in the average week? _____

2. Make a list of the outside commitments you have. Include professional, social, and community commitments.

   _____

   _____

3. Did you choose to work during a scheduled family activity in the past month? For example, did you work on a day when your son or daughter was playing in a soccer game?

   _____

4. When was the last time you had an hour alone with yourself with no demands?

   _____

5. Do you have all the latest time-saving devices? For example, do you have a fax machine or a car phone?

   _____

6. Do you ever feel things are happening too quickly? _____

7. Do you feel guilty if you aren't doing something? _____

8. What would you like to be doing if you weren't so busy? _____

   _____

   _____

9. Do you feel like you're too busy? _____

10. Do you need to check your calendar before you can agree to do anything?

    _____

DOES BUSYNESS EQUAL SUCCESS?

An unusual thing happened in the 1980s: we attributed success to people who were busy. The more hours you could say you worked, the more you were respected. That's the opposite of how it has been throughout recorded history. In the past, a sign of success was your ability to have time that wasn't committed. Having leisure time, the time to contemplate the world and the time to ask questions like "Why am I here?" was considered a sign of success. But not today.

To equate success with busyness has created problems. After a decade of trying to accomplish more, we are suffering the consequences: increased stress, illness, and alienation from loved ones. The list goes on. These are symptoms of a life that is out of balance.

Look at the word *busyness*. Just one small change—from Y to I—and you have a significant cause of the problem: business...work. Constant activity alienates you from yourself. You become too busy to know who you are or what you stand for. You have trouble setting priorities because you don't take time to clarify your values. If you think there is something missing in your life, you won't find what it is by doing more. Increasing the activity in your life will only hide it from yourself.

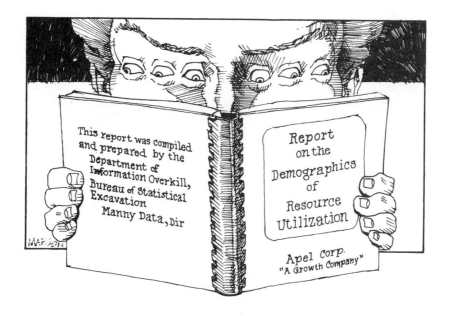

This report was compiled and prepared by the Department of Information Overkill, Bureau of Statistical Excavation
Manny Data, Dir

Report on the Demographics of Resource Utilization

Apel Corp.
"A Growth Company"

PARADOX: Less is more

WHAT DO YOU ENJOY?

You may be so busy that you don't take time to do the things you enjoy. It's easy to fall into automatically doing what needs to be done, what you committed yourself to yesterday. A steady diet of this and you begin to lose touch with the things that bring pleasure and joy. Life can come to feel like a lot of have-to's instead of want-to's. If you've forgotten what you love to do, it will be harder for you to identify your passion. Let go of some of your busyness and take the time to record the things that you enjoy.

Make a list of at least five things you enjoy in each of the following categories, and then add any other categories you wish.

Sports/Recreational

1. _____
2. _____
3. _____
4. _____
5. _____

Outdoor Activities

1. _____
2. _____
3. _____
4. _____
5. _____

With Friends

1. _____
2. _____
3. _____
4. _____
5. _____

With Family

1. _____
2. _____
3. _____
4. _____
5. _____

Alone

1. _____
2. _____
3. _____
4. _____
5. _____

Your Category _____

1. _____
2. _____
3. _____
4. _____
5. _____

How often do you do the things you enjoy? Weekly? Monthly? Yearly? What excuses do you make to yourself for not doing the things you enjoy? If you don't take time for the things you've listed, you may go after thrills and excitement instead. Unfortunately, excitement is an addiction that gets harder and harder to satisfy. Enjoyment is deeper and more abiding.

WHAT ARE YOUR TALENTS?

We each come into this world blessed with specific talents or gifts. These are abilities we have that seem to come naturally. These gifts can be a clue to our purpose, in that they can help us fulfill whatever it is we believe we are here to do. Some examples are athletic ability, dexterity, musical talents, taste, artistic abilities, sense of humor, ease with people, comfort with numbers, and so on. Take time now to think about what your talents are. This is part of what makes you unique as a person. List at least five talents before you go on.

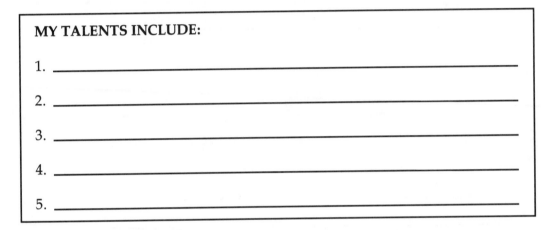

MY TALENTS INCLUDE:

1. _____

2. _____

3. _____

4. _____

5. _____

Did you have trouble with this exercise? Many people cannot identify five talents. They may never have taken the time to think about their talents, or they may not want to brag or boast. Don't worry! To acknowledge and own your talents will not send you on an ego trip. Quite the contrary: without this basic self-awareness, you can't make much of an impact on the world.

You may minimize or ignore your talents because they are things that come easily to you. You may assume that if it's easy for you, it's easy for everyone. This is a way you diminish yourself and mask your passion. If something comes easily to you, that's a clue that it's one of your talents.

OTHER PEOPLE'S IMPRESSIONS OF YOUR TALENTS

If you couldn't write down at least five talents, here is your next assignment. (You may want to do this even if you *did* identify five talents, because it is so rewarding and affirming.) Think of five people who know you very well. These could be friends, family members, neighbors, or colleagues. Arrange a time when you can speak with them alone, without being interrupted. Then ask them this question: ''What do you think makes me special? Do you think there is anything about me that is unique? What are my talents?'' Then listen and write down the answers they give you. When you have interviewed five people, look over all your notes and make a composite list. Write down the comments that were similar. Do the talents you listed match what your friends said?

Name _____

_____

_____

_____

_____

Name _____

_____

_____

_____

_____

Name _____

_____

_____

_____

_____

OTHER PEOPLE (Continued)

Name _____

_____

_____

_____

_____

Name _____

_____

_____

_____

_____

My composite list of talents:

_____

_____

_____

_____

WHAT ARE YOUR SKILLS?

Now that you've had a chance to think about your talents, let's take a look at your skills. A skill is something you *learned* to do. What competencies do you have as a result of training, experience, or education? Some examples include using computers, fixing an automobile, organizing, assertiveness, operating equipment, and time management. Most people have dozens of skills. Write down the skills you know you have. Then look at the list on the next page. It may trigger other skills you have and forgot to list.

MY SKILL LIST:

_____

_____

_____

_____

_____

You may discover that some of the traits you listed as talents are included on the following list of skills. That's because people often try to develop skills in areas where they do not have talents. For example, some people have a talent for organization. It is a gift and seems to come naturally to them. Other people have worked hard to learn organizational skills through taking seminars, reading books, or training on the job. You will need to make a judgment call about whether the traits listed are skills or talents for you.

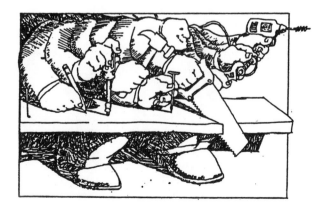

LIST OF SKILLS

Domestic:
- ☐ Cooking
- ☐ Cleaning
- ☐ Budgeting
- ☐ Shopping
- ☐ Gardening
- ☐ Decorating
- ☐ Repairing
- ☐ Raising children
- ☐ _____

Business:
- ☐ Organizing
- ☐ Planning
- ☐ Managing
- ☐ Delegating
- ☐ Computing
- ☐ Using office equipment
- ☐ Writing
- ☐ Accounting/working with numbers
- ☐ Speaking/training
- ☐ _____

Recreational:
- ☐ Golfing
- ☐ Swimming
- ☐ Hiking
- ☐ Reading
- ☐ Music
- ☐ Crafts
- ☐ Painting
- ☐ _____

Interpersonal:
- ☐ Listening
- ☐ Assertiveness
- ☐ Asking questions
- ☐ Motivating
- ☐ Selling
- ☐ Persuading
- ☐ Establishing rapport
- ☐ Negotiating
- ☐ Problem solving
- ☐ _____

Self-Management:
- ☐ Relaxing
- ☐ Positive thinking
- ☐ Time management
- ☐ Imagination
- ☐ Visualizing
- ☐ Following through
- ☐ Initiating
- ☐ Risk taking
- ☐ _____

This is not intended as an all-inclusive list of skills. It is designed to remind you of roles you play in your life and the skills you might use in these various roles.

MERGING YOUR TALENTS AND SKILLS

Is there any relationship between your talents and your skills? Have you developed skills that build on your gifts? For example, you may have natural athletic abilities, but have you developed any specific skills such as tennis? Or maybe you have a gift for writing. Have you developed skills in your use of language? Perhaps you have a natural eye for colors that go together. Have you developed any skills in interior design or wardrobe planning? You can make maximum use of your talents by developing skills around them.

Your unique blend of talents and skills is a clue to your passion.

In the chart below, record your list of talents and the skills you have developed around each talent.

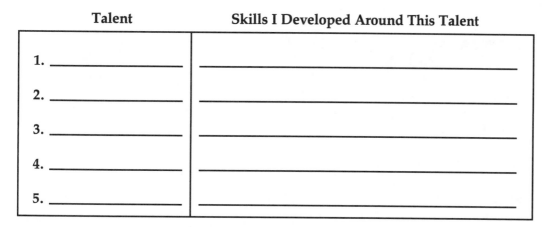

Talent	Skills I Developed Around This Talent
1. _____	_____
2. _____	_____
3. _____	_____
4. _____	_____
5. _____	_____

Remember the parable of the talents? Don't bury your talents, but instead cultivate them. This may mean you need to develop some skills to take your talents into the world. The more you use your talents, the more you will discover that life flows easily. You can let go of the struggle.

R FOR BUSYNESS: CULTIVATE SOLITUDE

> The creative person is constantly seeking to discover himself, to remodel his own identity, and to find meaning in the universe through what he creates...His most significant moments are those in which he attains some new insight, or makes some new discovery; and these moments are chiefly, if not invariably, those in which he is alone.''
>
> Anthony Storr, *Solitude*

If busyness is preventing you from knowing your passion, what can you do about it? You can cultivate solitude. Instead of complaining about how busy you are and how you don't have time to do the things you want to do, focus your energies on creating time for yourself.

Creative geniuses have always required and cherished significant time alone. Creativity cannot emerge when your mind is cluttered with business and busyness. Your greatest thoughts and ideas will come in times of quiet, reflection, stillness. This is a key to uncovering your passion. Remember, your purpose is not something you can think through and figure out. Instead, it is something that you feel, experience. It comes from deep inside of you.

Imagine yourself trying to talk on the telephone while a jet flies overhead, a rock band plays at a party in the next room, and a child cries next to you. It would be difficult, wouldn't it? And so it is with hearing your purpose. Your life may be so busy that it drowns out your inner voice. You don't need to make your inner voice louder; it is already perfectly clear. You need to turn down the volume in your life so you can listen to your inner voice.

CULTIVATE SOLITUDE

How can you cultivate solitude? There are many ways to accomplish this. Listed below and on the next page are some of the most common ones. Read through each one and put a check in the box if you could make this a *regular* part of your life. Solitude is not something that you do once a year! Ideally, you need some quiet time every day. During times of transition or when you need to make important decisions, you may need longer periods of solitude.

☐ **Walks.** Every day, take a walk alone, or silently with another person, for at least 20 minutes. During this walk, focus your attention on the present moment. Try to breathe slowly and deeply. Notice the trees, flowers, the feel of the wind on your skin. What color is the sky? What is the temperature? Use each of your senses to help you stay in the present.

☐ **Journal writing.** Each day, record how you feel, what you are thinking about. There are many ways to keep a journal. One of the best models is Ira Progoff's as described in *At a Journal Workshop*. For a journal to be most valuable, you want to record the process and flow of your life, not just the contents. In other words, don't just list the day's events; address the significance of those events, your feelings about them, or your reactions to them. If you don't interpret events, you will miss the great potential of journal writing as a means of self-discovery. It doesn't matter if you use notebook paper, a blank book, or a special journal format. What's important is that you do it on a regular basis.

☐ **Meditation.** There are many types of meditation, but they all have some elements in common. One method is to spend at least 20 minutes once a day sitting quietly, allowing your mind to grow still. You will usually have a word (called a mantra) or your breath as a point of focus. As you direct your attention, other thoughts will gradually drop away. As you begin practicing meditation, you will notice yourself going through several stages. First, you will find it is difficult to quiet your mind. As you learn to do this, you will notice that you can manage your stress better. You will feel calmer, more centered. As you continue in your practice, you will discover more about yourself and become increasingly aligned with your purpose. Meditation is one well-known path to spiritual growth.

CULTIVATE SOLITUDE (Continued)

☐ **Reflection.** It is so easy to lose sight of your life in the midst of living it. Alan Lakein coined the phrase "What is the best use of my time right now?" to help people manage their time. You may want to use this same technique of a focusing question to help you stay on purpose. Here are some possibilities:

How am I making a difference?

Is what I'm doing right now on purpose?

Is this what I really want to do?

Am I following my passion?

You may need a cue to remind yourself to ask one of the focusing questions. One way to do this is to go to an office supply store and buy a package of colored adhesive dots. Place these dots in several different places in your office and home where you are likely to see them. Then, whenever you see a dot, stop for 60 seconds and reflect on your life, using one of the above questions or others that you create. If you don't like the answers you give yourself, you may need to make some changes.

☐ **Quiet Time.** This is time, usually by yourself, when you eliminate outside distractions. Turn off the radio and television, ask family and friends not to disturb you, unplug the phone. In this atmosphere of quiet you can do any personally satisfying activity—sewing, exercising, taking a bath, shooting baskets, watching the sunset, working on a hobby. Quiet time gives you an undistracted opportunity to think.

☐ **Retreats.** In times of transition you may need more solitude than usual. Some transitions you expect—marriage, job changes. Others come as a surprise—divorce, death. When you reach one of life's choice points it can help to have some extended solitude. A night or a week away can be just what you need. Many people find that if the retreat allows them to be outside in nature, it is more healing than if they are confined to an indoor space.

Retreats are usually most effective when you go alone. However, it is also possible to go with someone and decide in advance that you will be silent with each other for a certain part of the time. For example, you might be silent from the time you wake up until dinner time. Just as we sometimes need to clean our closets of accumulated clutter, so we need to cleanse our minds with silence.

It is very easy to fill your life with activities, to be busy all the time. You may even be praised and admired by others for all you can do. But busyness can never lead you to your purpose. That's an inside job. Solitude balances the busyness with time for yourself. How willing *are* you to listen to yourself? You can't know your passion until you do.

MASK #2: WHAT WILL OTHER PEOPLE THINK?

> Your first obligation is to carry out the mission you are meant for, not what your father, mother, mate, or friends say you should do. Your mission will manifest in you when you decide to listen to your heart's desire.
>
> Naomi Stephan, *Finding Your Life Mission*

MASK #2: WHAT WILL OTHER PEOPLE THINK?

Write down here what you secretly think you would really, really like to do.

Why aren't you doing it? Could it be that you're worried about what other people will think?

Too often people know what they want to do, but hesitate to do it because of what other people might think. How often do you, before making a decision, ask yourself what someone else will think of the decision? There is a difference between consulting with someone to get their opinion and consulting to receive their approval. The latter can paralyze you. If you try to please all the others in your life, you will discover that it's not possible. It's not very fulfilling, either! Take a moment now and ask yourself who the others are in your life that you try to please.

Whom I try to please:

ARE YOU PLEASING YOURSELF?

Now think back over decisions you made in the past month. Did you make any of them based on what someone else would think, or did you make them to please yourself? How do you feel about each decision? An example is completed for you.

Example: I bought wallpaper that was more expensive than I planned for because I thought the decorator would think I was cheap if I didn't. It put me under some financial pressure and I regretted my decision.

Decision #1 and how I felt:

_____

_____

Decision #2 and how I felt:

_____

_____

Decision #3 and how I felt:

_____

_____

THE TYRANNY OF THE SHOULDS

If you look carefully at each of the statements you wrote down on the facing page, you will see that hidden within it is a *should*. In the example, the hidden should is ''Everyone should like and approve of me.''

You are probably well aware of how damaging shoulds can be to your self-esteem. They lead to feelings of guilt, inadequacy, and blame. You may even have invested time and energy releasing some of your shoulds. Nonetheless, people rarely recognize the enormous power that shoulds have to control their behavior and self-perception. More often than not, there is a should between you and your purpose, between you and self-acceptance, and between you and peace of mind.

There are three layers of shoulds: Having, Doing, and Being. Here are some examples of each type.

Having Shoulds

You should have: A nice car

A good job

Money in the bank

The latest clothes

Doing Shoulds

You should: Act your age

Volunteer in your community

Learn to swim

Listen to the news

Being Shoulds

You should be: Perfect

Strong

Smart

Successful

You may already have let go of the Having Shoulds and perhaps even some of the Doing Shoulds. You might even be tempted to skim over this section, thinking to yourself that you've heard all of this before. But have you let go of your Being Shoulds? These go so deep that you may not have questioned them. Yet they form the criteria upon which you judge yourself and decide whether or not you are okay.

THE TYRANNY OF THE SHOULDS (Continued)

Despite the pain and limitations that Being Shoulds impose on your life, they are extremely difficult to let go. Why? Because they were forged when you were a very young child, and they have come to define you. They provide a formula—although an often impossible one—for acceptance. The terror of releasing them is this:

Who are you if you are not your Being Shoulds?

To let go of your Being Shoulds, you need to take responsibility, in the profoundest sense of the word, for yourself.

Shoulds will limit and constrict your life. But more importantly, they can kill your spirit. If you should ''act your age'' (Doing Should), will you ever be able to go to an amusement park and delight in the rides? If you should ''be responsible'' (Being Should), can you ever take a risk? If you should ''be modest'' (Being Should), can you accept your gifts and talents?

What are your shoulds? Include Having, Doing, and Being Shoulds, but pay particular attention to Being Shoulds.

My Having Shoulds:

_____   _____

_____   _____

My Doing Shoulds:

_____   _____

_____   _____

My Being Shoulds:

_____   _____

_____   _____

When you let shoulds guide your life, you are living from the outside in instead of from the inside out. In other words, you give others control over your life. They have the power to decide whether you think you are okay or not. It gets very complicated when the various others in your life don't agree about what you should do. No matter what you decide, you suffer feelings of guilt, inadequacy, and unhappiness because someone thought you should do something else.

The only way you can be happy is to determine what *you* believe is right and to behave in a way that is consistent with that belief. You may not always please others, but you will please yourself.

Most important, when you live inside out, you are able to follow *your* purpose, rather than someone else's notion of what you should do. Your brothers and sisters may have worked in the family business, but if you feel called to study art, you will be happier and make a greater contribution if you listen to your calling than if you try to placate the family shoulds.

Reaching your higher self, your spiritual self, requires letting go of shoulds and doing the hard work of knowing yourself. Are you ready to let go of your shoulds and replace them with something that will serve you better?

℞ for Concern About What Other People Will Think: Determine Your Values

As the shoulds fall away, you will replace them with values. Values are beliefs that you choose to guide your life. A key word here is *choose*. Shoulds are absorbed without conscious choice. Values guide you in separating right from wrong in situations. When someone tells you what you should do, you can check his or her should against your values and decide what is right for you.

Not everyone will share your values. Do you judge people when they hold a different point of view? When it comes to values, there is no right or wrong, good or bad, there is only different. As you stop judging yourself, you will stop judging others. When the judging is silenced, you will be able to hear with increasing clarity what it is you really, really want to do.

Most of us can say in a minute what we should do, but it is far more difficult to articulate what we value. Look back over your list of shoulds. Are any of them values for you? Write down in the space provided any shoulds that actually reflect values you have. To shift your shoulds to values, you will need to change the way you talk to yourself. Instead of saying, ''I should do volunteer work'' (which creates guilt), try saying, ''I choose to donate time to community service.'' Other words you can use to replace your shoulds are ''I want'' and ''I prefer.''

Should   Value

_____   _____

_____   _____

_____   _____

_____   _____

All the values you have as an individual make up your personal value system. You may have fooled yourself into thinking you behave according to your values. In fact, many people find that it is extremely difficult to do what they believe is right, especially when faced with opposition. For example, you may say you value time with your family, yet you agree to work overtime whenever you're asked, because you ''should'' be a team player. To be truly value-led demands integrity and responsibility. Rather than taking a stand for their values, most people slide back to listening to their shoulds. You can guard against this by being clear with yourself about what you do value.

VALUES CLARIFICATION

Listed below are different values. For each one, rank how important it is to you on a scale of 1 to 10, with 10 being the most important. Then rank your behavior—how well you live your value—using the same scale. If the numbers are more than three points apart, use the third column to write down what action you need to take to bring your behavior and your values into alignment.

For example, you may rate your physical health as 10, extremely important to you. However, you do not exercise, you smoke, and you eat many high-fat foods. Your behavior you rate a five. In the third column your action plan might read, "Walk 20 minutes three times a week." You can modify your behavior or adjust your value to bring the two into alignment. Use the blank spaces to record any values you hold that aren't listed.

Value	Importance	Behavior	Action Step
Achievement			
Aesthetics			
Affection			
Altruism			
Appearance			
Arts (music, painting, writing, etc.)			
Authority/power			
Autonomy/personal freedom			
Career/employment			
Community			
Creativity			
Emotional health			
Environment			
Expertise			
Family			
Home			
Honesty			
Integrity			
Learning			
Leisure time			

Value	Importance	Behavior	Action Step
Love	_____	_____	_____
Loyalty	_____	_____	_____
Meaning	_____	_____	_____
Money	_____	_____	_____
Openness	_____	_____	_____
Personal Growth	_____	_____	_____
Physical Health	_____	_____	_____
Pleasure	_____	_____	_____
Privacy/solitude	_____	_____	_____
Recognition	_____	_____	_____
Relationships	_____	_____	_____
Religion	_____	_____	_____
Risk taking	_____	_____	_____
Security	_____	_____	_____
Service	_____	_____	_____
Socializing	_____	_____	_____
Spiritual	_____	_____	_____
Status	_____	_____	_____
Wisdom	_____	_____	_____
_____	_____	_____	_____
_____	_____	_____	_____
_____	_____	_____	_____

As you went through the list, did you notice that there are some values to which you assigned a low rank, yet much of your behavior is directed toward those values? That's a clue that shoulds instead of values are controlling your behavior! People often commit their time, energy, and resources to activities that are not congruent with their professed values. For example, you might have ranked service as low, yet you serve on committees in your community and church, and anytime someone calls looking for volunteers you say yes. Your resources (time, energy, money) are limited. Remember that when you say yes to something, you are saying no to everything else! Clarifying your values helps you make wise choices and escape the tyranny of the shoulds. Saying yes to your passion means saying no to your shoulds.

SELECT YOUR MOST IMPORTANT VALUES

Select the six most important values from your list on the preceding page, and give an example of that value in action during the past week. An example is given for you.

Value: *Honesty*

Example: *When my husband asked if I would like to go out for pizza, I told the truth and said I'd rather stay home.*

Value: _____

Example: _____

_____

Value: _____

Example: _____

_____

Value: _____

Example: _____

_____

Value: _____

Example: _____

_____

Value: _____

Example: _____

_____

Value: _____

Example: _____

_____

Did you have difficulty with this exercise? Until you put your values into action, you won't be able to create the life you want. When your behavior is in alignment with your values, you earn integrity.

REPLACE SHOULDS WITH VALUES

Some of the shoulds on your list may not reflect your values at all. In fact, they may be in direct opposition to your values! One of the best ways to let go of these shoulds is to replace them with value statements. Look back at the list of shoulds you recorded earlier. Some of them were, in fact, values that you converted by changing your language. But the other statements do not represent what you believe. Record them in the left-hand column below. In the right-hand column, write down the value you want to live by. See the examples before you begin. Please notice that you will need to decide *for yourself* which shoulds are not values. Different people will make different choices.

SHOULD	VALUE
I should make a certain amount of money.	*I want to do meaningful work regardless of what it pays.*
I should spend time on the weekend with my relatives.	*I want time alone on the weekends.*
I should clean my house and mow my lawn.	*I prefer spending time with my children to home maintenance and will hire someone to do these tasks.*
I should buy a new car.	*I prefer spending my money on travel rather than transportation.*
_____	_____
_____	_____
_____	_____
_____	_____
_____	_____
_____	_____

This process has just helped you eliminate meaningless shoulds and unnecessary guilt. You have made an active choice about what is important to you and what you believe. Now, whenever someone pulls a should on you, you can check their should against your values. If there is a match, great! Change the should into a choice and feel the increased sense of personal power. If the should does not coincide with your values, let it go and refocus on your values. This will free you from Mask #2, What Will Other People Think?

VALUE CONFLICTS

Sometimes you may have two values that seem to compete with each other. Then you need to decide which of the two is more important. These are usually difficult choices. Imagine that security is a high value and so is service. You may work as a volunteer providing services to the needy in your community while your partner works at a high-paying job. This arrangement allows you to honor each of your values without conflict. But suppose your partner is laid off and cannot find employment. Then what happens to your values? You may find yourself in conflict between your service and your security values. You will need to choose which value is higher for you. There is not a "right" answer. There is only *your* answer.

The only time you can compromise a value is for a higher value. For example, you might value loyalty and truth. What would you do if your boss asked you to do something that you believed was deceitful? If you compromise your values for any reason other than a higher value (because it would be easier, for example), you will lose your self-respect. It is not long after that that you lose your self-esteem.

Value conflicts are painful. They demand that you go deeper into yourself to find your own truth. They can be internal, interpersonal, or cultural. Look back through your list of values. Are you experiencing any value conflicts? Write them in the spaces provided.

Internal Value Conflicts

Example: Do I work on the book manuscript this evening (meaningful work) or spend time with my husband (family relationships)?

_____

_____

Interpersonal Value Conflicts

Example: *Do I express how I'm feeling (honesty) and risk being excluded (sense of community)?*

_____

_____

Cultural Value Conflicts

Example: *Do I landscape my yard like the other homes where I live (aesthetics, relationships) or do I use the money toward my child's college fund (family)?*

_____

_____

How have you resolved these dilemmas for yourself? Are you still struggling with some of them? The ultimate solution to a value conflict is contained in the following paradox:

*P*ARADOX: *The only way out is through.*

CREATE OR REACT?

This all boils down to who will be in charge of your life. Will you create the life you want, a life that is consistent with the values you hold? Or will you allow others to control you with the tyranny of the shoulds? If you do the latter, you will spend your time reacting and responding to what others want, never completely satisfying them or yourself. If you're in this mode, you have less of a chance of ever fulfilling your individual purpose. And isn't that why you're reading this book?

Write down here what you now think you really, really want to do.

_____

_____

_____

_____

_____

_____

_____

_____

_____

_____

_____

_____

_____

MASK #3: I'M NOT _____ ENOUGH

Everyone has his own specific vocation or mission in life to carry out a concrete assignment which demands fulfillment. Therein he *cannot* be replaced, nor can his life be repeated. Thus, everyone's task is as unique as is his specific opportunity to implement it.

Victor Frankl, *Man's Search for Meaning*

MASK #3: I'M NOT ___ ENOUGH

Are you beginning to realize that with each mask you are peeling off the ways you have stopped yourself from knowing or fulfilling your purpose? This third mask addresses how inadequate we can sometimes feel when we try to meet what we're called to do. In what ways do you feel you're ''not enough''? Write down all the reasons that come to mind.

I'm not _____

_____

_____

_____

_____ enough.

More often than not, you *feel* as if you aren't enough, when in fact you are. Remember the story *The Wizard of Oz*? The Tin Man, Scarecrow, and Lion were all seeking something they didn't believe they had. A funny thing happened when they got to Oz and met the Wizard. They each discovered that they already had what they were seeking! They hadn't acknowledged it. Is it possible that you, too, have all that you need?

In the spaces provided, think of three situations in which you *were* ''enough.'' It might help to think of times when you believe that you made a difference in some way.

I was ''enough'' when:

_____

_____

I was ''enough'' when:

_____

_____

I was ''enough'' when:

_____

_____

Now look back at how you filled in the blank ''I'm not ___ enough.'' In any of the three situations you just wrote about, did you have enough of that something that you think you lack?

THE COMPARISON TRAP

Sometimes you don't feel "enough" because you're comparing yourself to someone else. The Comparison Trap is very seductive because sometimes you "win." In other words, sometimes you come out smarter or more talented or better in some way. Unfortunately, you usually lose and feel inadequate, or less than, the other person. Look again at how you're not enough and ask, "Compared to whom?"

I'm not _____ enough compared to _____.

I'm not _____ enough compared to _____.

I'm not _____ enough compared to _____.

I'm not _____ enough compared to _____.

What did you discover? Are you making comparisons? The sooner you stop comparing yourself to others, the sooner you will be on your way to knowing and living your passion.

A belief that you're not enough, or not adequate, is an indication of low self-esteem. To let go of Mask #3, you will need to raise your self-esteem.

℞ for I'm Not ___ Enough: Develop Self-Esteem

Self-esteem is how you feel about yourself. You either like yourself or you don't. If you don't like yourself, it will be very difficult for you to trust yourself enough to listen to your inner voice, which will tell you what your passion is. If you do listen to yourself, with low self-esteem you probably won't risk acting on your knowing. You won't feel you're "worth it."

In Mask #1 you were asked to list your talents and skills. Very often people with low self-esteem have difficulty identifying their talents. They find it hard to believe that they are unique. Was it hard for you to list your talents?

SELF-ESTEEM INVENTORY

Here is a list of statements that people with high self-esteem tend to mark true. Read through each statement and mark it either *True* or *False*.

T	F	
☐	☐	1. I can admit a mistake.
☐	☐	2. I can reach out to people I don't know.
☐	☐	3. I maintain my values even when others don't approve of them.
☐	☐	4. I can accept a compliment without feeling uncomfortable.
☐	☐	5. I can be myself around other people.
☐	☐	6. I accept myself with all my faults and weaknesses.
☐	☐	7. I can tell you my strengths.
☐	☐	8. I can feel joy for someone else's achievements.
☐	☐	9. I do not compare myself with others.
☐	☐	10. I have peace of mind.
☐	☐	11. I believe I am unique.
☐	☐	12. I can let my inner child out and play without worrying about what others will think.
☐	☐	13. I accept differences in others without judging them.
☐	☐	14. I affirm myself and others.
☐	☐	15. I openly express my love for others.
☐	☐	16. I love myself.
☐	☐	17. I accept all of my feelings.
☐	☐	18. I enjoy my own company; I am comfortable being alone.

The more *True*s you have, the higher your self-esteem. If you had less than 13 *True*s, you may want to build your self-esteem* using the exercises that follow on the next several pages.

---

*For an excellent book on this topic, order *Developing Self-Esteem* using the form in the back of this book.

SELF-TALK

You talk to yourself all day long. In fact, you've been talking to yourself as you read this book! During these internal conversations, you may be planning, worrying, rehearsing, or remembering. As you engage in these thoughts, you might also be judging yourself. For example, if you're planning, you may think "I don't know how to do this, I'll never figure it out." If you're remembering, you might think "Why did I say that—it was such a stupid thing to say." Or perhaps you're worrying with thoughts like "I bet I don't get the promotion because I'm not as experienced as the other candidates."

It is these judgmental thoughts that cause feelings of low self-esteem. What you say to yourself affects how you feel about yourself. For the next hour, pay attention to your self-talk. Jot down in the space provided what you say to yourself. Then carefully review it. As Dorothy Briggs, author of *Celebrate Yourself,* says, "Are you in the building business, or the wrecking business?"

MY SELF-TALK

_____

_____

_____

_____

_____

_____

Keeping a self-talk log is similar to keeping a time log or a food journal. It lets you see in writing what you're saying to yourself. Once your self-talk is on paper, you can analyze it for shoulds, judgments, and other negative thoughts. Reading what you've written down can bring a painful awareness. Yet, until you know what you're doing, it isn't possible to change.

After you become aware of how you judge yourself, you can move to the next step, which is to say "Stop!" when you catch yourself starting to judge. With some practice, you will become very good at blowing the whistle on yourself! Then you can begin replacing the judgment with positive self-talk.

DAILY ACKNOWLEDGMENTS

How often have you gone to bed at night rehearsing in your mind the mistakes you made, the errors in judgment, the words spoken that were better left unsaid? When you do this, you erode your self-esteem. To increase your self-esteem, try giving yourself a daily acknowledgment instead.

A daily acknowledgment consists of taking a few minutes before you go to bed to recount to yourself 10 things you did that you feel good about. These do not need to be grand accomplishments! The quality of your life is measured by the little things. Reflect back over the day for all the positive things you said or did. If you fall asleep remembering the things you feel good about, you will awaken feeling good about yourself.

The following example of one person's daily acknowledgments will help you with the kinds of things to include. Take a moment right now to write out your daily acknowledgment list for today. You can add to it tonight if you like. The following two pages may be photocopied for your personal daily acknowledgment journal. At the end of each week, review your daily acknowledgments for the entire week—all 70 items! As your list grows, your self-esteem will grow!

DAILY ACKNOWLEDGMENT JOURNAL

1. I got out of bed when the alarm went off.

2. I took time to pet the cat before I left for work.

3. I kissed my partner goodbye and said ''I love you'' with feeling.

4. I let three people merge into my lane while I was on the freeway driving to the office.

5. I returned two phone calls without procrastinating.

6. I said ''thank you'' when the mail carrier dropped off my mail.

7. I gave someone my full attention when I listened to him or her.

8. I turned the TV off when the show I wanted to watch was over.

9. I ate an apple for dessert instead of cake.

10. I hung up my clothes instead of draping them over the chair.

MY PERSONAL DAILY ACKNOWLEDGMENTS

1. _____

2. _____

3. _____

4. _____

5. _____

6. _____

7. _____

8. _____

9. _____

10. _____

MY PERSONAL DAILY ACKNOWLEDGMENTS

1. _____

2. _____

3. _____

4. _____

5. _____

6. _____

7. _____

8. _____

9. _____

10. _____

YOUR UNIQUENESS

As you gain clarity about your purpose, you will discover that it has a synergistic effect on your self-esteem. Once you realize you are here on a mission that only you can perform, you find there is no need to compare yourself with anyone else. Everyone has a unique mission to fulfill. Each person will fulfill his or her purpose using his or her own personal set of talents and skills. How and where you use your gifts to fulfill your purpose will depend upon your personal life experiences. No one else on the planet is exactly like you.

As you raise your level of self-esteem and love yourself, you will come to know yourself better and to know what makes you unique. This knowledge will help you fulfill your personal purpose. You will bring to bear all of your life experiences—good and bad, all of your talents, all of your skills, and all of your hopes to make an impact on the world.

Take some time to reflect on the following questions. Use what you have discovered so far about your skills, talents, and values to help you. If you don't have an answer now, it's okay. Let yourself absorb the questions over time, and the answers will emerge.

1. How am I unique?

_____

_____

2. What skills and talents make me unique?

_____

_____

3. How have I used my uniqueness to affect my world?

_____

_____

4. How does my personal set of life experiences enable me to make a difference in the world?

_____

_____

5. When have I made a difference?

_____

_____

6. How did I do it?

_____

_____

7. Is that a clue to my uniqueness?

_____

_____

8. When have I felt most alive, energized, and present to the unfolding of my life?

_____

_____

9. Deep in my heart, why do I believe I'm here?

_____

_____

*P*ARADOX: *The question is the answer.*

AFFIRMATIONS

Another strategy you can use to build your self-esteem is that of giving yourself affirmations. This is the final step in the process of changing your negative self-talk. The first step was to become aware of what you say to yourself with the self-talk log. Then you practiced interrupting the thought with the word "Stop." The second step was to record your daily acknowledgments focusing on the positive instead of the negative. Now you will construct positive statements, or affirmations, that will eventually replace your negative self-talk.

With an affirmation, you affirm (in the *present*) something you want to create in your life in the *future*. Remember, you are today who you thought you were yesterday! In other words, if you've been telling yourself you'll never find the right job, you are probably working right now at something that you don't find fulfilling. If you continue to think the same way, you'll continue to get the same outcomes. However, you can change this pattern if you change your thinking. If you start today to affirm that you have meaningful work (assuming you don't already), you will create that outcome for yourself in the future. Napoleon Hill was right when he said, "If you think you can, or you think you can't, you're right."

Make statements to yourself that reflect the life you want. As you make these statements, keep in mind these rules for affirmations:

Rule #1: *State them in the present tense.*

Your behavior tends to mirror what you believe. When you state something to yourself as if it were true today, your behavior will come into alignment with the belief more quickly than if you state it as being true in the future. For example, if you are looking for a new job, you will not get as positive a result saying "I will find a good job" as you would if you affirmed "I have the job I desire."

Rule #2: *State them positively.*

Your mind can work more effectively with affirmations that express what you want rather than ones that express what you don't want. For example, "I accept myself" is more powerful than "I don't criticize myself."

Rule #3: *Use them every day.*

As you know, you talk to yourself all day long. Your affirmations need a chance to be heard in the midst of all the negative self-talk. Say them frequently, but say them at least every morning and every evening. If you say your affirmations as you fall asleep at night, you will be programming your subconscious mind when you are relaxed and more susceptible to suggestions.

Rule #4: *Empower your affirmations with feeling.*

When you say your affirmations to yourself, evoke as much feeling as you can. This is like supercharging your affirmation. You remember things that you feel. Recall a favorite movie or book. You probably remember it because it touched you on a feeling level. Express your affirmation with feeling and you will create it faster!

Your affirmations can be about anything. You might start, however, with affirmations related to your self-esteem. The more you like yourself, the more you will trust yourself and the more likely you are to share your gifts with the world. Below are some sample affirmations. Using these as a starting point, write your own. You will want to start with no more than two or three. As you bring these into reality, you can add others.

1. I now accept myself.

2. I am everything I need.

3. Every day, in every way, I am growing more and more healthy.

4. I let go of negative thoughts.

5. I am a loving person.

6. I love and respect all of my natural abilities.

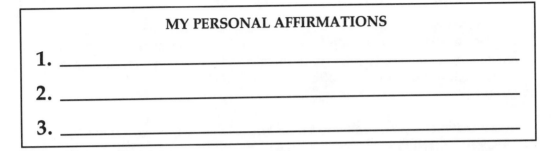

MY PERSONAL AFFIRMATIONS

1. _____

2. _____

3. _____

Now check what you have written against the four rules for affirmations. If you need to make any changes to what you wrote, do that now.

As with daily acknowledgments, you will begin to notice a difference after about one month of using affirmations. You will be pleased with the results.

I am coming to realize that my purpose is:

_____

_____

_____

_____

_____

_____

_____

_____

_____

_____

_____

_____

MASK #*4*: FEAR

Not only does every individual have a prophetic vocation, but...every individual has prophetic vocations. As times change and we change and our responsibilities in a changing culture change, we are called to let go sometimes of past prophetic calls and to immerse ourselves in new ones.

Matthew Fox, *Original Blessing*

MASK #4: FEAR

With the other three masks removed, you now reach the fourth reason why you may have hesitated to follow your heart. Are you afraid? There are two kinds of fear associated with your passion. First, you may be afraid to know what your passion is. Why? Because once you know, you are confronted with your responsibility to take action to follow your passion. You can allow yourself to be passive only as long as you ''don't know'' what you want to do. Most people want to be in control of their lives, yet few want to accept the responsibility that goes along with it, and they use fear to avoid knowing. Could this be true for you? Are you afraid to know the truth?

The second kind of fear occurs after you know what your passion is. This is the fear that is associated with taking a specific action toward fulfilling your passion. For example, you might need to go back to school and you may be afraid of this. In the space provided, write down as many of your fears as you can think of. Be as honest with yourself as you can.

I feel afraid to fulfill my purpose because:

_____

_____

_____

TYPES OF FEAR

Most fear falls into one of these five categories. Look at the fears you listed and put them into one of these categories:

Failure. Being laughed at, not doing it right, not knowing how to do it, making a mistake, not being capable.

My fears of failure:

_____

_____

Success. Being overrun with the success, losing friends because of it, overworking or becoming a workaholic, gaining notoriety, being consumed, having too much responsibility.

My fears of success:

_____

_____

I'll get hurt (physically). The stress of it will make me sick; it might kick up my ulcer; I'll have a panic attack; I won't be able to breathe.

_____

_____

I'll get hurt (emotionally/psychologically). They won't like me, I'll be rejected, I'll be excluded, I'll be embarrassed, I won't be able to cope, I'll make a fool of myself, my mate will leave me.

My fears of being emotionally hurt:

_____

_____

The unknown. I don't know what will happen, I don't know what to expect, I won't be able to cope with what happens, I won't know what to do.

My fears of the unknown:

_____

_____

UNDERSTANDING FEAR

Fear is an uncomfortable feeling. Consequently, people often try to hide their fear or to overcome it. But, like any other emotion, fear doesn't respond well to these tactics. It works better to understand and befriend the fear. How do you do this? You begin by recognizing fear as soon as it arrives. To do this, recall one of the fears that stops you from doing what you really want to do. Once you have the feeling clearly in mind, answer these questions:

Where do you feel the fear?
For example, fear lives in some people's stomachs. When they get the sensation of butterflies in their stomachs, they know it is present. For some, it lives in their legs. The expression *knees knocking* describes their fear. Now describe where your fear lives.

_____

_____

_____

If you were to draw a picture of your fear, what would it look like?
How big is it? What color? What shape? Is it abstract? Draw a picture of your fear in the space provided.

UNDERSTANDING FEARS (Continued)

What does your fear say?
List as many of its sayings as you can. This is especially important because it is often what fear says to you that prevents you from taking action toward what you really want. Once you learn what fear typically says to you, you can learn to talk back! Some people's fears say things like ''You'll be sorry! Don't do it! You can't! You'll fail.''

My fear says:

_____

_____

_____

How does your fear taste?
Be as descriptive as you can. Rather than saying ''bad,'' try to be more precise. For example, ''My fear tastes as bitter as a 50-mile-per-hour wind whipping my face on a –30° Minnesota winter morning.''

My fear tastes like:

_____

_____

_____

How does your fear smell?
Again, be as descriptive as you can. For example, ''The smell of my fear is noxious and clinging, like smoke clinging to fabric long after a fire is over.''

My fear smells like:

_____

_____

_____

By completing these questions you may discover that your fear is not as awful as you first thought it was. On the other hand, if it is truly a monster, now that you can see it clearly, you will be able to cope with it more effectively. The unknown is always more frightening that the known. You've just made your fear known to yourself!

LETTING GO IS SCARY

Fear occurs when you live in the future instead of the present—when you worry about what *might* happen. Look at the fears you listed above. Aren't they each related to something that *might* happen in the future? They are not present-moment realities.

Yet, to get to the future we often need to let go of the present. Fear is an emotion that accompanies the process of letting go. It's a sign that you are growing! The more attached you are to what you have, who you are, what you believe *today*, the more fear you will experience.

If you are invested in believing that you are smart, bright, quick to understand, then you will experience fear at the invitation to grow into areas in which you have little knowledge. You will need to let go of being knowledgeable and take on the role of learner. But if you're attached to your self-image, you will be afraid of becoming a student. If you're attached to your view of yourself as in control, you will be afraid to let go of control. Being vulnerable and trusting someone else will scare you. If you're attached to your good-paying job, you will be afraid to let go—to try work that promises more fulfillment.

Growth is a continuing process of going beyond. It is not rigid; it is flexible. It changes. To find and fulfill your purpose, you will be called to let go of where you are and go beyond. Of what must you let go to move closer to your passion? What scares you about letting go?

WHAT I NEED TO LET GO	MY FEAR ABOUT LETTING GO

When will you feel fear? Usually at moments when you are about to stretch yourself toward new growth. It's a sign that you are entering a personal frontier. It is associated with uncertainty as well as a sense of adventure. There is risk involved. You have an opportunity to move beyond yourself. *If you aren't feeling fear before you do something, it is an indication that the task at hand is not big enough for you.* Think of fear as a reassuring signal that you are on the right course!

RESPONDING TO YOUR FEARS

How do you usually respond to your fear? Do you try to eliminate it? Overcome it? Deny it? Avoid it? Worship it? Befriend it? Research it? Ignore it? Talk about it? Take action? Take a minute now and record three times in your life when you felt afraid. In the second column describe how you coped with the fear.

FEAR	HOW I COPED
Situation #1	
Situation #2	
Situation #3	

Based on these three situations, I see that I tend to respond to fear by:

_____

_____

_____

BEFRIEND YOUR FEAR

Fear is not your enemy! If you befriend fear, it can be an asset to you. There is a tremendous amount of energy associated with fear. You have undoubtedly heard stories of people who showed superhuman strength when they were faced with fear. In research studies, students who felt some fear about taking a test did better than students who felt no fear. Your goal is not to *eliminate* fear, but to *harness* it.

Let fear be a catalyst for your growth!

Fear can be transforming or it can be constricting. You decide which one it will be for you. If it is to be transforming, you need to identify what you are afraid of and then look behind it for the growth that is trying to break through. Focus your attention on your goal and let go of where you are.

> What the caterpillar calls the end of the world, the master calls a butterfly.
>
> Richard Bach, *Illusions*

To support this transformation, you need to focus on what you want, your *goal*, rather than your *fear*. Then the goal, rather than your fear, will become your motivator! Use the energy the fear produces to take specific action steps that will bring you closer to your goal.

PARADOX: To eliminate fear, embrace it.

List your fears about following your passion in the left-hand column of the chart below. In the center column, write down what you want—your goal. In the third column, write the action steps you could take to achieve your goal. An example is completed to help you get started.

FEAR	GOAL	ACTION
People won't buy my book.	*To write a best-seller.*	*Write every day.*
_____	_____	_____
_____	_____	_____
_____	_____	_____
_____	_____	_____

For many people fear leads to being stuck, to settling for what is rather than risking what is possible. You cannot find your purpose, much less fulfill it, without befriending your fears!

℞ FOR FEAR: DEVELOP COURAGE AND TAKE RISKS

> Courage is not the absence of fear; rather it is the ability to take action in the face of fear.
>
> Nancy Anderson, *Work with Passion*

There is a skill associated with befriending fear, and that skill is risk taking. Like any skill, you get better at it with practice. How comfortable are you with risk taking? Complete the following questionnaire to find out. For each question answer yes or no.

RISK QUESTIONNAIRE
Y or N

_____ 1. I don't take as many risks as others might because I know my limits.

_____ 2. I seek others' approval before I take a risk.

_____ 3. I believe it's better to be safe than sorry.

_____ 4. I need to feel in control in most situations.

_____ 5. If some action scares me, I stop doing it.

_____ 6. I take a risk only if there's nothing to lose.

_____ 7. I feel uncomfortable with uncertainty.

_____ 8. I prefer to do things the way I've always done them.

_____ 9. I hate to make a mistake or be wrong.

_____ 10. I think things change too quickly.

_____ 11. I research any risk before I go forward with it.

_____ 12. I feel uneasy around people who take lots of risks.

_____ 13. I have trouble acting on what I believe.

_____ 14. I change my mind easily if other people disagree with me.

_____ 15. I can't remember the last time I took a risk.

_____ 16. I sometimes wish I had taken a risk in a situation.

_____ 17. The first thing I consider before taking a risk is what could go wrong.

_____ 18. I have difficulty asserting myself.

The more *yes* answers you have, the less of a risk taker you are. If you have more than nine yeses, this section will help you to increase your risk-taking behavior.

RISK TAKING

There are three types of risk takers.*

Nonrisk Takers. These people like to play it safe in all situations. If you fall into this category, you answered the Risk Questionnaire with at least 12 yeses. Nonrisk takers are unlikely to know their passion because to know it would demand that they take some action. Not knowing is much safer. If they do become aware of their passion, they complain about why they can't fulfill it. Complaining is safer than being responsible for their life. Chances are that if you are a nonrisk taker you feel powerless over your life.

Calculated Risk Takers. These people take planned risks. They consider the possible benefits as well as the probable consequences of an action. They weigh their alternatives before they act. They see mistakes as a learning opportunity, not a failure. They want to grow and stretch themselves. Calculated risk takers recognize that there are no guarantees and plan accordingly. Even as they go forward with a risk they have a plan B in mind in the event things don't go as they hope. They are not afraid to acknowledge when they make a mistake. Because of their careful planning, they often do not perceive their actions as a risk.

Impulsive Risk Takers. These people love the thrill of a risk! They like to live dangerously. They do not consider the downside of a risk. They wear blinders and see only the outcome they want. Often the important people in their life feel uneasy with many of their actions. For impulsive risk takers, the sense of danger is what gives them satisfaction, not achieving a specific outcome. If you answered *no* to all the questions in the Risk Questionnaire, you may be an impulsive risk taker!

---

*Consider ordering *Risk-Taking* using the form in the back of this book.

DAILY RISK BEHAVIOR

Before you take the big risks in life, you need to experience success with smaller risks. Take a moment now and record some of the risks you have taken in the past week. These do not need to be major, life-changing risks. Remember, you need to start small. If you can't think of five in the past week, list five in the past month.

1. _____
2. _____
3. _____
4. _____
5. _____

Did you have trouble making a list? To increase your risk-taking behavior, follow the advice of Bill McGrane, founder of the McGrane Self-Esteem Institute, who says, "Stretch yourself to be uncomfortable every day." Let's look at how you might do this.

You could:

1. Drive a new route to work.
2. Say hello first to people you meet on the street.
3. Smile at strangers.
4. Tell the truth sooner.
5. Apologize when you are wrong.
6. Compliment people when they do something you like.
7. Call someone you don't know but would like to meet and suggest getting together.
8. Tell someone you love, "I love you."
9. Do something silly.
10. Risk being embarrassed.
11. Ask what a word means when someone uses language you don't understand.
12. Do nothing for half an hour.
13. Speak out at a meeting.
14. Express how you feel.
15. Disagree with someone.

Using this list as a starting point, write down at least five ways you could stretch yourself to be uncomfortable in the coming week. Then do it! As you do, you will find yourself able to take bigger and bigger risks. As Iris Murdoch said, "At crucial moments of choice, most of the business of choosing is already over." If you don't learn to be a risk taker today, you won't be able to take a risk when you are faced with a big opportunity. Your moment will pass because you weren't ready.

Risks I will take:

1. _____
2. _____
3. _____
4. _____
5. _____

STEPS TO IMPROVE YOUR RISK TAKING

Step 1: Start small. As your comfort level increases, so will the size of your risks.

Step 2: Collect as much information as possible about the possible risk.

Step 3: Consult with other people. Note that this is different from seeking their approval.

Step 4: Ask yourself, ''What is the best possible outcome?''

Step 5: Ask yourself, ''What is the worst possible outcome?''

Step 6: Ask yourself, ''How likely is the worst possible outcome?''

Step 7: Ask yourself, ''If the worst possible outcome occurred, what would I do?'' If you don't have an answer for this question, this may not be a risk you want to take.

Step 8: Ask yourself, ''What is the probable outcome of *not* taking the risk?'' You may have forgotten that continuing to do what you're doing can be very risky. Your present course is not safer simply because it's familiar. For example, you may be considering changing jobs and think a new position is risky. But if you suffer from headaches or some other physical ailment in your current work, you may be risking your health if you *don't* make a change.

Step 9: Evaluate the outcomes of the risks you take. Did it turn out as you expected? If not, why not? What have you learned for the next time?

Step 10: Celebrate your successes. When you take a calculated risk and you achieve the outcomes you wanted, give yourself credit for taking a risk. Gradually you will come to see yourself as a risk taker.

MASK #5: THE HAVING MODE

Under the values that will guide this more temperate time, the hunger for more will certainly not vanish, but it can be redirected. More money, more tokens of success—there will always be people for whom those are adequate goals, but those people are no longer setting the tone for all of us. There is a new sort of more at hand: more appreciation of good things beyond the marketplace, more insistence on fairness, more attention to purpose, more determination truly to choose a life, and not a lifestyle, for oneself.

Laurence Shames, *The Hunger for More*

WHAT IS SUCCESS?

What is your definition of success?

_____

_____

_____

Describe three achievements in your life. Be specific about what you did, what you achieved, and what there was about the experience that made you decide it was a significant achievement.

Achievement #1:

_____

_____

_____

_____

Achievement #2:

_____

_____

_____

_____

Achievement #3:

_____

_____

_____

_____

What is the relationship between how you defined success and your achievements? Do you consider yourself successful?

LIFESTYLE OR LIFE?

The decade of the 1980s was a decade of greed. Life was characterized by more, more, and more, and measured by price tags and designer labels. What you did was less important than how much you were paid for doing it. Choosing meaningful work was less important than choosing work that paid well. Enjoying life took a back seat to having a lifestyle. Success was measured in dollars; your net worth determined your self worth. Materialism, consumption, having things all took the place of the inner work that is necessary for a life of meaning.

Are there any ways in which your lifestyle has taken on more importance than your life?

1. _____
2. _____
3. _____

People got confused. They thought that having things would make them happy. When they attained these things, there were two rude awakenings. First, having doesn't make you happy. The advertisers promised that when you had a particular car or lived in a particular neighborhood or dressed a certain way you would be happy. They lied. Happiness is an inside job. It comes from being who you are, fulfilling your purpose, and living your values. Things are empty sources for meaning.

What have you wanted that, once you got it, didn't give you the joy, satisfaction, or happiness that you expected?

1. _____
2. _____
3. _____

Second, things are not guaranteed. You can lose them. Thousands of people lost their jobs during the 1980s due to mergers, downsizing, and changing technology. When the jobs went, so did the lifestyle they were collecting. Others lost things when the stock market crashed in 1987. The realization dawned that things are transient; they can be taken away. Things are not a stable basis upon which to stake your happiness.

When are you the happiest?

_____

_____

Did your answer have anything to do with material possessions? The more disconnected and alienated you are from your self, your inner purpose, the more likely you are to look outside yourself, to material things, for meaning. As Matthew Fox wrote in *Original Blessing*, ''It is not letting go *of things* that is important, but the letting go *of attitudes* toward things.''

HAVE, DO, OR BE?

Eric Fromm in *To Have or To Be?* described a misconception that climaxed in the 1980s. He said people spend their lives trying to

> *Have* enough (money, resources, things) so that they can
>
> *Do* what they want (in terms of work, how they spend their time), because then they can
>
> *Be* happy.

Unfortunately, most people get stuck at the first step. They never "have" enough. Perhaps you've said to yourself, "When I have the car paid off I'm going to make a change." Then when the car was paid off you said, "After I have the kids educated, then I'm going to make a change." One day you reach the end of your life and realize you've never done what you wanted to do with your life.

Fromm says that to have a satisfying life you need to invert the formula. First, you need to

> *Be* who you are. Know your strengths, weaknesses, your purpose. This self-awareness will lead you to
>
> *Do* what you love. This doing will be the contribution of your unique gifts. Because you are giving yourself away, you will be rewarded, and
>
> *Have* what you need. Of course, there are no guarantees you will have everything you want! As Dick Leider says in *The Power of Purpose*, "There are two ways to be rich; one is to have more, the other is to want less." To reach the stage of having requires patience. While you wait, you need to define yourself by who you *are*, not what you *have*.

How do you turn the *having/doing/being* cycle around? You stop making having— money—the goal. You stop measuring success by your bank account and possessions. You get your priorities in order and follow your heart, guided by your values.

MISCONCEPTIONS ABOUT MONEY

1. **Money is the goal.**
   When money becomes the goal, as it has for so many people, it signals the corruption and deep loss of self. Life becomes trivialized. No amount of money or possessions can ever make you whole. Only living from your center can do that. Money is a reward for service; it is a byproduct of excellence.

2. **Money can make you happy.**
   Joy and happiness are feelings that come from the inside. They cannot be bought or possessed. These feelings come from a state of being, not of having. You can feel unhappy if you do not have enough money to meet your essential needs, but money is not sufficient to give you happiness. ''The fascination of simply making money wears thin in time. The real fruits of one's labors are seen in the planting of one's gifts.'' (Wexler and Wolf, *Good-Bye Job, Hello Me*).

3. **Money is what makes the world go around.**
   Sometimes it seems that way! Love, not money, is the true world currency.

4. **Once you have enough money, then you can do what you want.**
   The having mode is very addictive. Your definition of what ''enough'' is continually rises. Have you noticed that even before you get a salary increase your lifestyle is out ahead of it?

5. **Money = Success.**
   ''Making money is a private affair, but success, so to speak, is by general consent; we all of us define it every day. We have a right to demand a real accomplishment, a making of something better, before we give someone our regard and our applause.'' (Laurence Shames, *The Hunger for More*). Money is a byproduct of success.

6. **Money makes you powerful.**
   Money gives you privilege, not power. Real power comes from within. It is an energy you share with others. Power that comes from the outside can be easily lost if others withdraw their support. Because of the addictiveness of the having mode, it is easy to begin taking more than you give. When that happens, the very people who put you in power can take you out of power. Even well-to-do people can feel anxious and uneasy if they lack a center.

7. **Money makes you free.**
   Money is usually spent on possessions. Think for a minute about what you have done with your money. Are you surrounded with things that you need to care for, keep clean, keep safe? Consumption becomes a trap, not freedom.

℞ FOR THE HAVING MODE: SHIFT TO THE BEING MODE

The having mode is certainly seductive. But by definition having is possessing, and it can disappear as easily as it came. The being mode is not so transient. In this state you are centered, authentic, connected to your spiritual self. You have your personal power to assist you in creating and fulfilling your passion. If you can comfortably be yourself (without living from your "shoulds"), your need for outside approval disappears.

From the centered place of being, your vision of who you are can express itself. You will be *drawn* to your passion. In the having mode, you feel *driven*. It is no coincidence that you hear about being "market-driven" or even "value-driven." These concepts come out of the having mode. The language of purpose is "value-*led*" or "customer-*led*." What feels better to you, being led, or being driven?

Think back over times when you have felt inspired—times when you were drawn to a person or idea. Recall situations in which you thought to yourself, "I'd like to make that kind of impact." When you felt inspired you may have noticed that you reacted physically with shivers up your spine, or tears of awe. Describe three situations when you felt inspired.

1. _____

_____

_____

2. _____

_____

_____

3. _____

_____

_____

As you reflect on those situations, were you pulled to take any action? Your passion can be an inspiration to you if you let it be.

QUALITIES OF BEING

If is difficult to understand what it means to *be*. We spend more of our time *doing* or *having*. As you review the following list of *being* qualities, put a check mark (✔) beside the ones you have experienced. Put an X in the box beside the qualities you would like to develop.

✔ or X

□   1. **Discipline.** A discipline is something you do every day, whether you feel like it or not, without concern for where it's getting you. To commit yourself to a discipline puts you on the path of mastery. Examples of disciplines could include keeping a journal, meditating, playing an instrument, or practicing a martial art. Discipline is not something you *have*, discipline describes who you *are*. Your state of being will grow with discipline. As you cultivate solitude, the ℞ for Mask #1, you will simultaneously develop discipline. Viktor Frankl's words are the paradox for the fifth mask:

*P*ARADOX: *What is to give light must endure burning.*

QUALITIES OF BEING (Continued)

☐ **2. Responsibility.** You are responsible to your purpose; to bring it into reality. This is not a responsibility *for*, but a responsibility *to*. Your ability to respond comes directly from the state of being. To be yourself requires action; it is not a passive state.

☐ **3. Be yourself.** Can you be with yourself quietly, alone? If you can't be with yourself, you probably don't accept yourself. And if you can't be with yourself, how can you let anyone else be? You'll want to spend time and energy changing them. Most importantly, if you can't let yourself be, you will find it extremely difficult to express your being—your passion.

☐ **4. Present to the moment.** Being occurs only in the now, this moment. To *be* demands that you stop living in either the past or the future. When you are in the moment, you are open to life as it unfolds. This present awareness allows you to see and take advantage of opportunities as they present themselves. When you are able to stay in the now you will notice you feel less fear and experience less stress.

☐ **5. Awareness.** Do you say "I have a problem," or do you say "I feel troubled?" The second phrase is from a state of being. You are aware of how you feel. You are aware of yourself in relation to the rest of the world. Rather than possessing your experience, you are aware of your experience. When you think in terms of having or possessing, the next logical step is to control, conquer, or overcome. Today our relationship with the environment is a classic example of the negative effects of this way of relating to the world.

☐ **6. The observing self.** Ironically, as you increase your awareness, stay more present to the moment, and develop the other qualities of being, you will discover that you have a level of consciousness that observes all of this. Even as you read and complete the exercises in this workbook, there is a part of you that can observe you. This aspect of your self is pure consciousness, the eternal I AM.

☐ **7. Vision.** Your passion is the expression of who you are. No one else can be you better than you can. Your unique expression in the world comes from being yourself. If you begin the search for your purpose by asking what pays well, you will miss your potential for vision. The more you are able to *be*, the more clarity you will have about your purpose.

WHO ARE YOU?

Answer this question 20 times. Resist the temptation to answer the question with what you do or what you have. Try to stay in the being mode.

I am:

1. _____

2. _____

3. _____

4. _____

5. _____

6. _____

7. _____

8. _____

9. _____

10. _____

11. _____

12. _____

13. _____

14. _____

15. _____

16. _____

17. _____

18. _____

19. _____

20. _____

WHAT IS YOUR PURPOSE?

Now that you have worked through the five masks, your purpose may be very clear. If it is not yet completely clear, you undoubtedly have a better idea of what it is, and you know which areas (masks) you need to continue working with so that your purpose becomes clear. Be patient with yourself!

Write out your personal statement of purpose as you now understand it in the box at the bottom of this page. You might want to include the following parts in your statement: first, use a verb to describe your purpose (serve, teach, train, write, create, counsel, make, sell, etc.). Then choose a noun to describe who or what (children, the elderly, consumers, the earth, the poor, computers, etc.). For the next part, include the skills or talents that you will use (you identified these in the exercises in Mask #1). Finally, include the outcome that you want. Here are a couple of examples to get you started.

Examples:

1. My purpose is to teach adults how to read, using my love of words, books, and ideas, so that people will be more confident in their day-to-day living.

2. My purpose is to strengthen families, using my counseling skills to help adults be better parents.

Notice that the same purpose could be expressed in many ways. This allows for the growth and change that will occur throughout your life. Thus, a purpose of teaching could change over time from adults to employees at XYZ Company to volunteers at ABC Agency. Even the purpose itself could change. Remember what Matthew Fox said in the quote at the beginning of Mask #4: ''We are called to let go sometimes of past prophetic calls and to immerse ourselves in new ones.''

My purpose is:

In the box below, draw a symbol for your passion as you understand it at this moment. There are no right or wrong answers. If your passion remains unclear at this moment, symbolize your search.

Now, describe what you drew. If you need help with this go back to the early section where passion was likened to a flame. Then fill in your description.

My passion is like _____

(what you drew)

because _____.

(explain)

P A R T

III

New Truths In A Life Guided By Purpose

Passion doesn't come from business or books or even a connection with another person. It is a connection to your own life force, the world around you, and the spirit that connects us all. You are the source.

Jennifer James, *Success Is the Quality of Your Journey*

NEW TRUTHS IN A LIFE GUIDED BY PURPOSE

The secrets for success are well known: drive, persistence, goals, control, focus, and so on. The secrets for finding your purpose are not as well known. You might think of the secrets of success as being the "old truths." The secrets to living your life "on purpose" are the "new truths." The new truths include: process, trust, intuition, paradox, ecology, creativity, levels of truth, patience, and flow. In this final part of the book, three of the new truths will be explored—process, intuition, and paradox.

FROM GOALS TO PROCESS

"Don't be so greedy for the fruit that you miss the flowers."

You have been told over and over that reaching the goal is what counts. The destination is the ultimate aim. But have you ever noticed that reaching a goal doesn't always bring the joy and satisfaction that you had expected? Look back at the exercise you completed in Mask #5. There you listed examples of goals that didn't bring you the satisfaction you expected.

Goal attainment can be shallow because it is the *process* of accomplishment that gives life meaning. It is the striving, the searching, the seeking, the yearning that is the thrill! It is not the arriving. A goal simply sets the direction, and that's all it is intended to do. If you mistakenly put all your focus on the end result, you will miss your life! Rather than being present to the moment, you will have lived your life in the future. Life occurs in the *now*.

If you focus on goals exclusively, on those occasions when you *do* achieve them, you probably won't take the time to savor your accomplishment. Instead you'll be rushing on to the next project. Do you celebrate your achievements?

THE JOY COMES FROM THE JOY-NEY!

The importance of process was portrayed beautifully in the Academy Award–winning film *On Golden Pond*. In it, Henry Fonda spent the summer trying to catch a big fish. Over time, he got his grandson (Doug McKeon) involved in the search for the big fish. They used a variety of baits and tried different times of day and areas of the lake. Finally they caught him. McKeon was thrilled and was ready to have the fish for dinner. But Henry Fonda wanted to let the fish go. He explained to the confused youngster that the joy was in the *search* to catch the big fish. *Having* it was not the objective. McKeon finally understood and they released the fish.

As you move from the having mode to the being mode, you shift your focus from goals to process. Very simply, process is the *how* of things, not the *what*. How often have you said, "It's not what she said, it's *how* she said it," or "It's not what he decided, but how he decided it?" The process, the how of our lives, matters a great deal.

> Remember, when you can, that the definition of success has changed. It is not only survival, the having—it is the quality of every moment of your life, the being. Success is not a destination, a place you can ever get to; it is the quality of your journey."
>
> Jennifer James, *Success Is the Quality of Your Journey*

Process is not linear. It is circular. You're going to have an opportunity to experience this now by completing a life-cycle exercise. Begin by watching an internal movie titled "This is MY Life." Think back to where you were born, your family of origin, first childhood memories, early school experiences, adolescence, first love, high school years, college days, first job, significant relationships, marriage, children, disappointments, achievements, and relationships with family and friends. Watch your movie until you reach the present moment of sitting here reading this book.

On the facing page is a large circle. At the top is birth and also death. Recalling the movie you just watched, record the significant experiences in your life on your life cycle. Try to include 20 to 25 items.

YOUR LIFE CYCLE

> We shall not cease from exploration, and the end of all our exploring will be to arrive where we started and know the place for the first time.
>
> T. S. Eliot

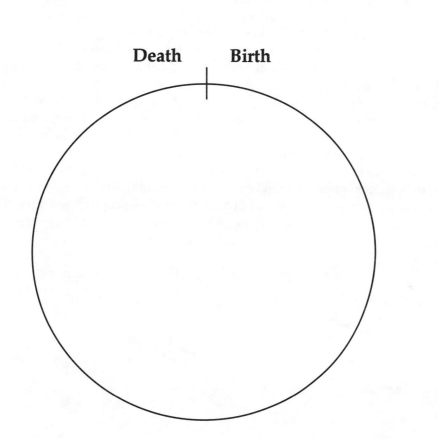

STEPPINGSTONES—YOUR LIFE PROCESS

You have just completed a chronology of your life by recording events that have happened during your lifetime. Now you're invited to get in touch with the *process* of your life. You're going to take that two-dimensional circle and lift it up to become a three-dimensional spiral!

Look back at the experiences you recorded. Now go inside yourself and ask: In a word or two, how would I describe the *flow* of my life? In other words, how have you experienced your life subjectively? The objective is to go deeper than the reporting of events, to the meaning they had for you. For example, two women could each have spent six years at home raising children. But the meaning of that experience can be completely different for each woman. One might describe those years as "I was trapped," while the other might describe the experience as "I was nurturing." These process descriptions are a far more intimate expression of your life than a mere chronology. Another person would know much more about you by listening to the flow of your life than by listening to the chronology of your life. Notice also that in the example above a woman might have on her life cycle "Caitlin born, Scott born, Collin born." Yet when she thinks about the *process*, all three chronological events are part of a single time—being trapped or nurturing. This is what is called a steppingstone. As you look at your life cycle, try to remember how you felt. Here are a couple more examples to get you started.

> *"I went to college, was selected to participate in a special intern*
> *program, and traveled to another part of the country to study."*
> (chronology)

> *"I learned."* (process)

> *"My husband and I separated and finally divorced."* (chronology)

> *"I was bitter."* (process)

YOUR STEPPINGSTONES

Below is a spiral with circles representing steppingstones. Narrow the 20–25 chronological events in your life cycle into no more than 10 steppingstones. Write the words that you would use to describe the process of your life on each steppingstone. Try to feel how one process, or steppingstone, flowed into the next. Read through your list of steppingstones quietly to yourself to feel the flow and movement in your life.

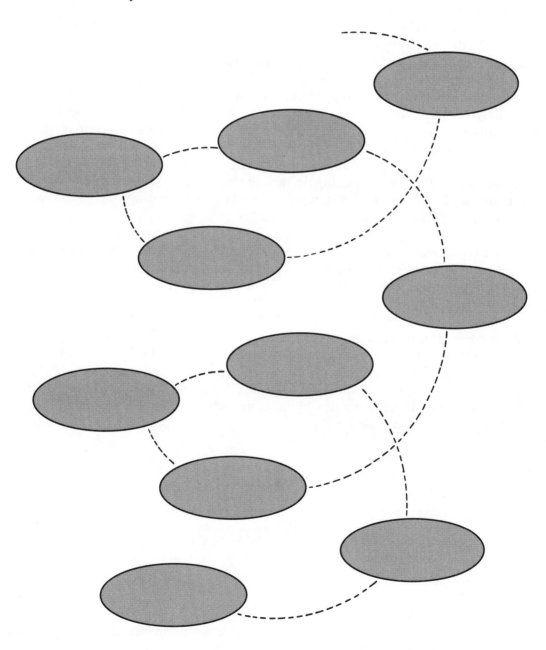

EXPLORING YOUR STEPPINGSTONES

Did you start at the top of the page or the bottom of the page as you wrote down your steppingstones? In other words, do you perceive your life as climbing or deepening?

Notice the thin line that connects the steppingstones and makes the spiral. This is the common thread that is working its way through your life. Have you allowed each experience to lead you to the next in your life? Can you see that who you are and what you are doing in your life at this moment would not be possible if you had had a different set of life experiences? The challenge is to use life's experiences as *steppingstones* and not as bricks that form walls.

The spiral also allows you to see, graphically, the growth process. Before there is any movement forward, there is movement backward. In your life this can feel like you are losing ground or like you are stuck. Such times are better understood as times of inner growth. Think about the daffodils that bloom in your garden. Before they can flower in the spring, they need a period of dormancy, when it appears that nothing is happening. In fact, the bulb is preparing itself to flower. You are like the flower. You, too, need a period of time to grow yourself into your next step. Such times can feel dark and bleak.

Process is organic. It demands that you trust yourself and trust something greater than yourself. There is not a moment when your growth is complete; it continually unfolds, flows, until we die. To see life merely as a series of goals is to miss it entirely.

When you shift from goals to process, you allow your life to happen instead of trying to control it or make it happen. To accept your life as an art that is in process demands patience. You need to be able to wait. This is not easy, especially in a culture that demands a quick fix. Solitude, the ℞ for Mask #1, will help you develop patience. Practicing a discipline, as described in the ℞ for Mask #5, will also help you develop patience.

You can see that most of your steppingstones encompass a period of months, if not years. Rarely does your life change dramatically from one day to the next. It takes patience to see that the gentle, gradual movement in your life is what enables you to grow. As you trust the process and develop patience, you will dramatically reduce your stress. Finding your purpose is a process that takes time. Reading this book in one hour will not give you The Answer. This book is describing what the process is so that you can have a companion and some guidance on your journey. From soul searching to clarity to action may take you years!

As you look at your steppingstones, notice also that, in order for you to move to the next steppingstone, you needed to let go of where you were. You cannot move forward in your growth without being willing to grow beyond where you are. Remember the exercise in Mask #4 on letting go? When you have difficulty letting go, your spiral will get larger. At other times you will be aware that your spiral is very tight; change and growth occur quickly then. If you're holding on, growth will be slower than if you take the risk to let go.

Breakthroughs occur when you can let go. Your patience will serve you well here, too. Sometimes you will need to wait before you let go. For example, you may need to put more pieces in place before you quit your current job!

This leads us to a paradox of the journey:

***P**ARADOX: Every act of creation is an act of destruction.*

INTERNAL TIME/EXTERNAL TIME

Process occurs in a different dimension of time than your chronological life. Process functions on internal time, which can be faster or slower than clock time. To get a sense of this for yourself, answer these questions.

When did time seem to fly by? What were you doing? Why do you think it seemed to go so fast?

_____

_____

_____

_____

When did time drag? When did it seem to pass at a snail's pace? What were you doing? Why do you think it seemed to pass so slowly?

_____

_____

_____

_____

When did time stop? When did you totally lose any sense of time? When have you had the experience of an endless ''now'' moment? What was different about this experience from times when time flew or dragged?

_____

_____

_____

_____

Your answer to the third set of questions is a clue to moments when you have been in a state of being, rather than a state of having or doing. Your passion emerges from being and is an expression of your being.

FROM LOGIC TO INTUITION

Most people intuitively know what it is they really want to do. As you worked through the exercises of the masks, you may have noticed that you had a hunch or a gut feeling about your purpose. You may have heard a quiet voice whispering to you, telling you what your purpose is. This voice is your inner knower, or your inner wisdom. Were you listening? Or do you discount this way of knowing?

You will not "figure out" your passion; it is not something that the logical mind uncovers. Your purpose will come to you through another channel, your intuition. At its most developed level, intuition is your connection to a higher level of consciousness. Jung called this the *collective unconscious*. Mystics have called it God. The purpose of removing each of the masks is to enable you to better hear your inner knower. The new truth is not only to listen, but to take action on this knowing. How often have you said after something happened, "I knew it!" But you didn't trust what you knew! This level of consciousness is the source of creativity. Intuition is the sixth sense that allows you to know things you could not know with your rational mind.

Every person is intuitive. Many people, however, do not listen.

Take a minute right now to think back over times when your intuition talked to you and you did not listen. What was the outcome? Do you wish you had listened? Look back and remember three times when you wish you had listened to your intuition.

1. I wish I had listened to my intuition when _____

_____

because _____

_____

2. I wish I had listened to my intuition when _____

_____

because _____

_____

3. I wish I had listened to my intuition when _____

_____

because _____

_____

BLOCKS TO INTUITION

Why didn't you listen to your intuition in the examples you just wrote down? Probably because of distrust, fear, or external listening.

DISTRUST

To trust your intuition, you need to believe in yourself and trust yourself. The ℞ for Mask #3, developing self-esteem, will help you do this. If you aren't confident in your inner wisdom, you'll depend too heavily on logic, analysis, and other cognitive, rational processes. There is nothing wrong with a left-brain approach to situations. By itself, however, it does not give you the complete picture. When you trust your intuition, you get more of the truth. And you get it much faster than when you use your intellect!

Would you listen to a person you didn't trust? Probably not. In fact, you would actively tune him or her out. The same thing happens when you don't trust your intuition. You drown it out with busyness, thoughts, analysis, preoccupations. It is no surprise that some people claim they have no intuition; they've spent years denying, ignoring, and distrusting it.

It is uncomfortable not to be able to articulate why you know something or how you know it. That's why intuition requires trust. You need to make a leap of faith and trust that this way of knowing is as valid as any other. The more you trust your spouse or loved one, the more they tell you about themselves, and the better you get to know them. The more you trust your intuition, the better you will get to know it, too.

Intuition also demands your trust because it presents you with pieces. You rarely get all the parts at one time. You need to trust that, as you continue down the path, more pieces will be revealed to you. If you like to be in control (old truth), this is very difficult!

FEAR

Some people try to silence their intuition out of fear. They are not afraid of what their intuition might say, but rather that they might need to *do* something if they listened to their intuition. Once you are aware of what needs to be done, it is hard to respect yourself and maintain high self-esteem if you don't take action. Are you afraid to act on what you know?

You may realize intuitively, after working through the five masks, that your passion is landscaping. If you currently work as an accountant, you are in an uncomfortable situation. To be true to yourself, you need to take some action, no matter how small. Your integrity is at stake if you don't.

It is so much easier, so much safer, to say to yourself, ''I know I'm not happy in my work, but I just don't know what I want to do.'' Then you can safely ''study'' the situation. You get ready to know rather than risk knowing.

Be honest with yourself now! What do you know, but hesitate to admit to yourself, because of the action you would need to take?

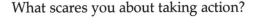

_____

_____

_____

What scares you about taking action?

_____

_____

_____

_____

_____

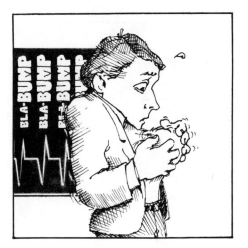

BLOCKS TO INTUITION (Continued)

EXTERNAL LISTENING

How often have you discounted your intuition because it didn't agree with what someone else thought? Do you put more credibility in your friends' opinions than in what you intuit? Do you try to meet other people's expectations instead of listening and following your inner knower? Do you relinquish your truth for someone else's truth?

To avoid these traps, take action on the R,s outlined in Masks 1, 2, and 3. First, take time alone, to know what you want, how you feel (the R, for Mask #1). Second, identify your values (the R, for Mask #2), and last, develop your self-esteem so that you can risk being different (Mask #3).

When people in a group withhold their personal opinions to support the opinion of the group, a phenomenon called Groupthink occurs. This is a very dangerous situation for companies, because without the contributions of individuals, unwise decisions are made and opportunities are missed. When you let someone else dictate the decisions you make about your life, you put them in control. When you go along with others, you betray your own inner wisdom. Each betrayal is a silencing of your intuition. Eventually you only listen externally. Internal listening keeps you open to your intuition.

When did you let someone talk you out of trusting your intuition?

_____

_____

How did it turn out?

_____

_____

DEVELOPING YOUR INTUITION

There are several steps you can take to develop your intuition. The first is to let go of the blocks to intuition that were just described. Then you can turn up the volume of your intuition by using the following techniques.

PREPARATION

Your intuition puts pieces together into a whole, but it needs the pieces to do this. The more information, learning, and experience you gather, the more your intuition has to work with to create an intuitive ''flash.'' True expertise is the blending of knowledge, experience, and intuition. For example, if you have been working with computers for the past 10 years, attending conferences, and reading about your field, you will have a better chance of intuitively solving a computer problem than someone who has limited experience, hasn't kept current in the field, and isn't as knowledgeable.

Soil that is well prepared sprouts more seeds than soil that is poorly prepared. Your intuition follows the same principle. The better you prepare yourself, the more your intuition will flourish.

INCUBATION

When a seed is planted, it needs time to germinate before it sprouts and breaks the soil. We tend to get impatient with this process. We want it now. We try to force it. Intuition cannot be forced; we need to *allow* it. You have undoubtedly had the experience of trying to solve a problem, but try as hard as you might, no answer came forth. Later, while you were taking a shower or driving somewhere, the answer magically appeared as if from nowhere.

The answer needed time to incubate. After you prepare your mind by giving it everything you know about the problem, you need to give your intuition time to work on it. Assume an attitude of openness to receive the answer your intuition offers.

DEVELOPING YOUR INTUITION (Continued)

AHA!

This is the moment of awareness. The answer comes to you. Sometimes it seems obvious, but other times you may feel uncertain, hesitating to trust what you sense.

Intuition speaks to each person in its own way. Some people report that they experience their intuition as a feeling about something. Others describe a gut reaction. Some see an image or picture of what they need to do or have a dream. And still others hear a message. You need to acquaint yourself with how your inner knower communicates with you. This is important, because you can confuse wishes, hopes, and fears with intuition. Each of these is different.

Wishing and hoping are both *thoughts*. Intuition is not a thought, it is an instant, immediate knowing. There is no rational process.

In Mask #4 you wrote down a description of your fear. You used all five senses— how it feels, sounds, smells, tastes, looks. Sometimes you may wonder whether your intuition is talking to you, or whether you are just hearing your own fear. You can test what seems to be intuition against what you know is fear.

Think about times when you are aware that your intuition is talking to you. How does your inner knower communicate with you? Be as specific as possible. Then compare this with how your fear talks to you.

VERIFICATION

You need to test your intuition against reality. Try out the idea. See if it works. You may need to collect more information before you act on your inner wisdom. For example, you might get an intuitive flash to move to another part of the country. Before you sell your home and pack your bags, do some research.

This is true of your passion. Perhaps you're beginning to realize that you want to work with children. Before you quit your present work, investigate the types of work you can do with children, the training you'll need, and so on.

Intuition is at the root of most scientific breakthroughs. A person has an intuitive flash about the nature of the universe or about how something works. This is followed by the hard work of verifying the intuitive knowing. Science today is using sophisticated quantum physics to verify the intuitive knowing of mystics who lived centuries ago.

As you begin paying more attention to your inner knower, it can be valuable to keep an intuition log. First, record whatever you perceive as intuitive flashes or awarenesses. Then monitor and record how accurate you are in distinguishing intuition from wishes, hopes, or fears. You may discover that what you initially thought was intuition was really a wish. Over time you will become more skilled at discriminating between your thinking, wishing, hoping, predicting, or scared self and your intuitive self. Your intuition log will assist you in better understanding when and how your intuition speaks to you.

INTUITION LOG

Date	Intuition	Outcome

FROM EITHER/OR TO AND

Our linear approach to life creates dualism, or seeing things as either/or. Life, however, is not linear. It is circular. It is a continuing process. Everything cycles back around to itself. Winter and summer are not opposites; one leads to the other. When we realize this, we can see that rather than *either/or*, life is *and*.

Learning to see the *and* is not easy. It demands that we become comfortable with paradox. *Either/or* gives us a feeling of certainty and security. *And* is ambiguous and uncertain. *Either/or* limits our thinking; *and* expands it.

Dualism, or seeing things as opposites, creates separation—from ourselves, our work, each other, the environment. Paradox is about the connections, the unity of ourselves with others, with work, with the planet. Each way of thinking represents a totally different view of the world.

Science has contributed to a dualistic world view, especially in the past few centuries. Newtonian physics presented a mechanistic view of the world in which everything could be subdivided into separate, distinct parts. Over the centuries, the search for the one smallest building block of all matter led to quantum physics. This most advanced form of scientific research has proven that the basic building block of everything that exists is a particle *and* a wave! The essence of life is not *either/or*! It is *and*. Now science leads us into a paradoxical view of the world. These discoveries verify what mystics have been saying since the beginning of recorded history. There is unity and oneness. It is a paradox that we see separation.

The hologram is an excellent example of paradox. It is a two-dimensional object, yet when you look at it, it appears to be three-dimensional. A more common object is a rocking chair. You have undoubtedly sat in one, moving back and forth, back and forth—yet never getting anywhere!

How comfortable are you with paradox? Paradoxes have been sprinkled throughout this book to help you see that finding your purpose is not an either/or proposition. It emerges and you create it. It is analogous to the work of a sculptor, who has a vision to bring into reality through the medium of stone or bronze. Yet the medium itself will direct the creation. For his sculpture David, Michelangelo accepted a block of marble that had been rejected by previous sculptors because of a deep gash. The stone itself dictated the sculpture, and yet Michelangelo chipped away everything that wasn't David. From this process came one of the world's most beautiful sculptures.

From a state of being, your intuition will tell you your purpose. The next step is to bring your passion into reality. You become a cocreator as you go about the process of seeing the opportunities in your life to express your passion. The challenge for each of us is to create the vision we see in our hearts.

What follows is a list of paradoxes that apply to the journey. As you read each one, write down your personal experience with the paradox. Here is an example to help you get started.

Example:

The more things change the more they stay the same.

I felt dissatisfied in my work so I changed jobs. The new company was much better—for a while. Now I feel dissatisfied again. I realize that changing companies wasn't really making a change. I'm still doing the same thing!

_____

_____

_____

To gain control, relinquish it.

_____

_____

_____

To change others, alter yourself.

_____

_____

_____

Every ending is a beginning.

_____

_____

_____

To become a part of, grow apart from.

_____

_____

_____

The soul does not grow by addition, but by subtraction.

_____

_____

_____

102

To be secure, be vulnerable.

_____
_____
_____

The more I learn, the less I know.

_____
_____
_____

Add your own paradox: _____
_____
_____
_____

Finding your purpose is an inner journey. Only *you* can answer life's most demanding questions. Yet you have a companion—this book. Let these exercises guide you to deeper levels of awareness. The question of your purpose will not be answered once and for all. Rather, like the process we've described, the answer will emerge as you create it.

This journey you are on is literally your life. Savor it!

PARADOX: This solitary work we cannot do alone.

YOUR FEEDBACK IS IMPORTANT

This book is the result of feedback from participants at the author's seminars and retreats over the past several years. Your feedback is important, too! Please take a few minutes to answer the following questions.

1. The most important ideas for me were:

2. I would like to know more about:

3. I have made the following changes since reading this book:

4. I feel that I am/am not fulfilling my passion. My passion is:

5. Additional comments:

Please mail to:

Barbara Braham
Finding Your Purpose
C/o Crisp Publications, Inc.
1200 Hamilton Court
Menlo Park, CA 94025

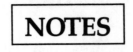

NOTES

FOR OTHER FIFTY-MINUTE SELF-STUDY BOOKS
SEE THE BACK OF THIS BOOK.

NOTES

FOR OTHER FIFTY-MINUTE SELF-STUDY BOOKS
SEE THE BACK OF THIS BOOK.

NOTES

FOR OTHER FIFTY-MINUTE SELF-STUDY BOOKS
SEE THE BACK OF THIS BOOK.

NOTES

FOR OTHER FIFTY-MINUTE SELF-STUDY BOOKS
SEE THE BACK OF THIS BOOK.

NOTES

FOR OTHER FIFTY-MINUTE SELF-STUDY BOOKS
SEE THE BACK OF THIS BOOK.

ABOUT THE FIFTY-MINUTE SERIES

We hope you enjoyed this book and found it valuable. If so, we have good news for you. This title is part of the best selling *FIFTY-MINUTE Series* of books. All *Series* books are similar in size and format, and identical in price. Several are supported with training videos. These are identified by the symbol **V** next to the title.

Since the first *FIFTY-MINUTE* book appeared in 1986, millions of copies have been sold worldwide. Each book was developed with the reader in mind. The result is a concise, high quality module written in a positive, readable self-study format.

FIFTY-MINUTE Books and Videos are available from your distributor. A free current catalog is available on request from Crisp Publications, Inc., 1200 Hamilton Court, Menlo Park, CA 94025.

Following is a complete list of *FIFTY-MINUTE Series* Books and Videos organized by general subject area.

Human Resources & Wellness (continued):

Communications & Creativity:

Customer Service/Sales Training:

Small Business & Financial Planning:

Adult Literacy & Learning:

Career/Retirement & Life Planning: